WHY YOU CAN'T BE A CHRISTIAN AND VOTE DEMOCRAT:

NO COMPROMISE

A Biblical Guide to Faithful Citizenship

PM Kimbler

BeaconLight Press

Copyright © 2025 PM Kimbler

All rights reserved. No part of this publication may be reproduced, distributed, or transmitted in any form or by any means, including photocopying, recording, or other electronic or mechanical methods, without the prior written permission of the publisher, except in the case of brief quotations embodied in critical reviews and certain other noncommercial uses permitted by copyright law.

Scripture quotations are from the King James Version (KJV). Public Domain.

Published by BeaconLight Press. For permission requests, contact info@beaconlightpress.com

First Edition ISBN: 979-8-9932513-1-8
Printed in the United States of America

DEDICATION

To every Christian who refuses to compromise God's truth for political comfort, and to those who are still searching for the courage to align their vote with their faith.

To the pastors who have forgotten that "all Scripture is profitable" and that Christ's lordship extends over every ballot box — may you find the courage to preach the whole counsel of God, not just the parts that keep pews filled and offerings flowing.

To those who declare "God is not political" while His Word speaks to every area of life — may you remember that silence in the face of evil is not neutrality; it is complicity.

And to my family, whose patience, sacrifices, and unwavering love carried me through the long hours and heavy burdens of writing—this work is dedicated as much to you as to the truth it proclaims.

"Choose you this day whom ye will serve… but as for me and my house, we will serve the Lord." — Joshua 24:15

ACKNOWLEDGMENTS

This book exists because faithful Christians throughout history have refused to separate their faith from their citizenship. I am grateful to those who have modeled biblical courage in the face of cultural pressure.

To my family, who supported me through the challenging process of writing uncomfortable truths. To my church family, who encouraged me to speak boldly when it would have been easier to stay silent. To the pastors and teachers who taught me that God's Word applies to every area of life, including the voting booth.

Most importantly, to my Lord and Savior Jesus Christ, whose authority extends over all things—including politics. May this book honor His truth and advance His kingdom.

"All Scripture is breathed out by God and profitable for teaching, for reproof, for correction, and for training in righteousness." — 2 Timothy 3:16

A NOTE TO READERS

This book will challenge you. It will confront assumptions you may have held for years about faith and politics. It will ask you to examine whether your vote truly reflects your beliefs.

Some will call this book divisive. Others will say it's too political for Christians to discuss. But the truth is never divisive—only our response to it divides us.

The Democratic Party has made their position clear through their platform and policies. Now you must decide: Will you follow Jesus completely, or will you find ways to compromise His truth for political convenience?

The choice is yours. But you cannot serve two masters.

"No one can serve two masters, for either he will hate the one and love the other, or he will be devoted to the one and despise the other." —Matthew 6:24

FOREWORD

There comes a time in every generation when someone chooses to courageously stand for the truth. Though the subtle lies and deceptions disguised as compassion may capture the minds and hearts of millions, a singular written work can be used by God to expose corruption in the highest governmental and cultural places. It is through the bold and daring pen of PM Kimbler in the pages ahead that the truth concerning the modern-day Democratic Party is revealed.

The increasingly anti-God positions held by Democrats over the past seventy years are blatantly exposed by the author, supported both by Scripture and historical events and facts. Intended as a wake-up call for all Christians who still vote Democrat, the objective of the writer is to emphasize the sanctity of the voting booth as a gift from God, not to be compromised.

The modest differences between the two major political parties in the 1950's have become so wide and incompatible in 2025 as to become the contrast between good and evil. What God calls evil the Democrats endorse and even sanction. The political warfare today has become a spiritual battle for the soul of America. The mainstream media and much of social media have become complicit in influencing public opinion in favor of policies that God calls abominations.

If doubt still clouds your thinking concerning the veracity of these claims, continue to read with an open mind as PM Kimbler unveils the darkness that pervades the Democratic

Party and allows the light of God's Word to shine on the truth that graces the pages ahead.

—R Adams
Streams in the Desert

FOREWORD

And for such a time as this, "Why You Can't Be A Christian And Vote Democrat!" by PM Kimbler.

We the People of God, the Church of the Living God, are being called upon to take a strong stand to not only acknowledge our God-given rights to govern and rule our nation, but to enforce them. For way too long we have heard from the pulpits call across this nation that God is not into politics, and that it doesn't matter who the president is because we have God! Yes, it's even been said that God is neither for government nor against government, because it's only about souls.

Well, if that's the case, then we must've missed the verse in the Bible that declares, "When the righteous are in authority the people rejoice; but when the wicked bear rule the people mourn" (Proverbs 29:2). And why would God even instruct us to pray for Kings and all who are in authority that we may lead a quiet and peaceable life in all godliness and honesty (1 Timothy 2:1-2), if God wasn't into government? In Hosea 4:6, God said, "My people are destroyed for a lack of knowledge because they have rejected knowledge."

The truth be told, the real reason for the condition of our nation is not because of the devil. It's because of the condition of the body of Christ. As goes the body of Christ, so goes the government, so goes the nation. Through ignorance and complacency we have forfeited our God-given rights to govern and rule. However, that day is over! The line in the sand is drawn and now is the time to decide whose side you are truly on! Choose this day to whom you will cast your vote! God versus the devil!

Just as God sent the prophet Elijah to the children of Israel who were backslidden and serving Baal, the prophet by the Word of the Lord said, "How long halt you between two opinions? If the Lord be God follow Him. But if Baal, then follow Him" (1 Kings 18:21).

Without any reservation there is no doubt whatsoever but that God likewise has given PM Kimbler this masterpiece, "Why You Can't Be a Christian and Vote Democrat." In this God-inspired book she methodically lays out the Democrat party's platform, without any exaggeration, exposing its rotten agenda to its core. She uncondemnly makes the case why you can't be a Christian and vote Democrat by comparing the anti-God platform of the Democrat party next to the Light of God's Word, which is without any controversy the ONLY standard and guide book whereby Christians should cast their vote.

For sure PM Kimbler in this book is saying the quiet part out loud! Actually she is undoubtedly shouting it from the roof tops! I believe wholeheartedly that God has given Patrice the same message as He gave to the prophet in Isaiah 58:1-2 to "Cry aloud, spare not, lift up your voice like a trumpet, and show my people their transgressions..."

Thank you, my blessed sister in Christ for the honor of writing this foreword.

John 15:8: "Herein is my Father glorified, that you bear much fruit."

—Pastor David Barnes

AUTHOR'S SPECIAL NOTE

In recent days, as I prepare this book for release, the reality of the times we live in has been made painfully clear. We have witnessed increasing acts of hostility, intimidation, and even violence from the extreme left toward those who dare to speak truth. The brutal assassination of Charlie Kirk is a sobering reminder of just how far this darkness is willing to go. His death is not an isolated incident — it is part of a larger spiritual war being waged against God's people, against His Word, and against anyone who will not bow to the idols of this age.

Let no one be deceived: this is not simply about politics. It is about light versus darkness, truth versus lies, and God versus the devil. When the left embraces godlessness, when their platform celebrates sin and mocks righteousness, violence inevitably follows. Jesus Himself warned us, "If the world hate you, ye know that it hated me before it hated you" (John 15:18).

This is why I wrote this book. The days of compromise are over. The line is drawn, and every believer must decide where they stand. These attacks only confirm the urgency of this message: we cannot separate our faith from how we vote, how we lead, and how we live. To do so is to surrender our God-given authority and open the door to the very destruction now unfolding before our eyes.

I offer this note as both a warning and a call. Do not be surprised when truth is met with hatred. Do not shrink back when evil shows its teeth. Stand firm, lift high the cross, and remember:

"When the righteous are in authority, the people rejoice: but when the wicked beareth rule, the people mourn" (Proverbs 29:2).

— PM Kimbler

TABLE OF CONTENTS

Introduction 1

Chapter 1: The Authority of Scripture 9
Chapter 2: Abortion and the Sanctity of Life 17
Chapter 3: Marriage, Sexuality, and Gender 27
Chapter 4: Economic Policies and Biblical Stewardship 39
Chapter 5: Religious Liberty and Free Speech 47
Chapter 6: COVID-19 55
Chapter 7: Social Justice and Biblical Justice 77
Chapter 8: The Role of Government and Biblical Authority 83
Chapter 9: Borders, Immigration, and Biblical Law 89
Chapter 10: The Test of True Faith 97
Chapter 11: A Call to Faithful Citizenship 103

Discussion Questions 109

Appendix A: What They Say vs. What the Bible Says 115
Appendix B: Key Bible Verses for Voting 119
Appendix C: Platform Comparison—Democrats vs. Republicans
.... 125
Appendix D: Resources for Christian Voters 127
Appendix E: How the Democratic Party Abandoned God 131
Appendix F: Your Biblical Voting Checklist 135

Scripture Index 139

Endnotes 151

Introduction

You're about to read the most important political book you'll ever encounter.

Not because it's written by a famous politician or Washington insider. Not because it promises easy answers or tells you what you want to hear. But because it confronts the most urgent question facing American Christians today—a question that will determine not just how you vote, but whether your faith is real.

Can you follow Jesus and vote Democrat?

Maybe you've been wrestling with this question for years. Maybe it's been keeping you awake at night. Maybe you've been told that faithful Christians can disagree on politics, that your vote doesn't define your faith, that Jesus transcends party lines.

This book will prove all of that wrong.

PM Kimbler

The Crisis of Our Time

We're living in the most spiritually dangerous moment in American history. Not because of external enemies or economic collapse, but because millions of people who claim to follow Jesus are supporting policies that mock everything He stands for.

They vote for unlimited abortion while claiming to love children. They champion same-sex marriage while saying they honor God's design. They support open borders that fuel human trafficking while talking about compassion. They back economic policies that punish hard work while quoting verses about helping the poor. They enable government overreach that shuts down churches while claiming to defend religious freedom.

This isn't just political disagreement—it's spiritual schizophrenia.

And it's tearing apart the church, confusing the culture, and destroying our nation's moral foundation.

What You'll Discover

In the pages ahead, you'll discover truths that will shake you to your core:

Why the Democratic Party's 2024 platform reads like a point-by-point rejection of biblical Christianity.

From their defense of late-term abortion to their war on religious freedom, their agenda attacks God's design for life, family, sexuality, government, and justice.

How Christian Democrats twist Scripture to justify supporting policies God clearly condemns.

You'll see their favorite verses taken apart and put in proper context, exposing the dangerous game of spiritual manipulation they're playing.

The Real-World Consequences of Abandoning Biblical Principles in Politics.

This isn't theoretical—people are dying, children are being trafficked, families are being destroyed, and the church's witness is being compromised because Christians are voting against their supposed convictions.

Why "My Faith is Private" is the Most Unbiblical Statement a Christian Can Make.

You'll learn why compartmentalizing your faith from your politics isn't humility—it's rebellion against Christ's lordship.

The Line in the Sand

This book draws a line in the sand that many Christians don't want to see.

On one side stands God's truth—unchanging, eternal, non-negotiable. On the other side stands the modern Democratic Party—promoting policies that directly contradict Scripture at nearly every major point.

You can stand on one side or the other. But you cannot stand on both.

That's What "No Compromise" Means.

It means you don't get to call Jesus "Lord" while supporting leaders who mock His teachings. It means you don't get to claim biblical authority while voting for policies that contradict it. It means you don't get to compartmentalize your faith when it becomes politically inconvenient.

It means following Jesus completely, or admitting you don't follow Him at all.

Why This Book Now

Some will say this book is too harsh, too political, too divisive. They'll argue that Christians should focus on the gospel instead of getting involved in messy political battles.

But here's what they're missing: This IS the gospel.

When Christians support policies that destroy innocent life, they're attacking the God who creates life. When they champion the redefinition of marriage, they're undermining the relationship that pictures Christ and His church. When they enable government to replace God as ultimate authority, they're promoting idolatry. When they justify these positions with twisted Scripture, they're doing exactly what Satan did in the Garden—questioning whether God really said what He said.

This isn't about Republican vs. Democrat. This is about truth vs. lies, biblical authority vs. human rebellion, Christ's lordship vs. cultural compromise.

The stakes couldn't be higher. Not just for America, but for the integrity of the Christian faith itself.

What This Book Is Not

This isn't a book about why you should vote Republican. It's a book about why you cannot vote Democrat if you truly follow Jesus.

This isn't about political strategy or winning elections. It's about spiritual integrity and biblical obedience.

This isn't about attacking people. It's about exposing dangerous ideas that are leading souls astray and destroying our nation.

This isn't about being mean or unloving. It's about loving people enough to tell them the truth, even when that truth is uncomfortable.

And this definitely is not about being politically correct. Political correctness is what got us into this mess in the first place.

What You'll Need

Reading this book will require courage. You'll be challenged to examine whether your political choices align with your claimed faith. You might discover that positions you've held for years contradict Scripture. You may need to change your vote, your party affiliation, or your entire approach to citizenship.

You'll also need humility. If you've been supporting Democratic candidates while claiming to follow Jesus, this book will show you why that's impossible. Admitting you've been wrong isn't easy, but it's the first step toward getting right with God.

Most importantly, you'll need to let Scripture be the final authority. Not your emotions, not your political preferences, not what your friends think, not what sounds nice or feels good. Just God's Word, clearly understood and faithfully applied.

The Promise

If you'll read this book with an open heart and mind, I promise you three things:

First, you'll gain crystal-clear biblical vision about political issues. No more confusion, no more internal conflict, no more wondering what Jesus would do. You'll know exactly how Scripture applies to the major political questions of our time.

Second, you'll understand why your vote is a spiritual issue. You'll see that politics isn't separate from faith—it's one of the most important ways you demonstrate what you really believe about God's authority.

Third, you'll be equipped to stand firm when the pressure comes. And it will come. When culture, media, and even some churches pressure you to compromise, you'll have biblical truth as your unshakeable foundation.

Your Moment of Truth

Every generation of Christians faces moments that test their faithfulness. This is ours.

Will we bow to cultural pressure, or will we stand on God's Word? Will we seek the approval of men, or the approval of God? Will we compromise for comfort, or choose courage for truth?

Your answer will be revealed not by what you say you believe, but by how you vote.

The time for fence-sitting is over. The time for half-hearted Christianity is done. The time for political compromise in the name of false unity has passed.

This is your moment of truth.

Turn the page, and let's discover together what it really means to follow Jesus with no compromise.

"How long will you waiver between two opinions? If the Lord is God, follow him; but if Baal is God, follow him." — 1 Kings 18:21

PM Kimbler

Chapter 1: The Authority of Scripture

A Call to Stand Firm

You're standing in the voting booth, ballot in hand, and your heart is racing. The question that's been eating at you for months finally demands an answer: Can I vote Democrat and still follow Jesus?

You've heard Democratic politicians talk about their faith. They quote Bible verses like "Love your neighbor as yourself" (Mark 12:31) to back up their ideas. They sound caring when they talk about helping people and fighting for justice. But something feels wrong. Deep down, the Holy Spirit is nudging you, whispering that things aren't what they seem.

Here's the hard truth this book will prove:

You cannot be a Bible-believing Christian and support today's Democratic Party. The two just don't mix.

Look at the facts. The Democratic Party's 2024 platform doesn't mention God even once. Not "God," not "Lord," not "Almighty"—nothing. This isn't an accident. They've deliberately turned their backs on the truth that Psalm 33:12 teaches: "Blessed is the nation whose God is the Lord."

Their actions prove what they really believe. They fight for unlimited abortion. They push ideas about marriage and gender that go against everything God created (Genesis 2:24; Matthew 19:4-6). They want to divide people by race instead of bringing them together in Christ.

Jesus warned us about this in Matthew 7:21: "Not everyone who says to me, 'Lord, Lord,' will enter the kingdom of heaven, but the one who does the will of my Father who is in heaven." Can faith that supports these policies really be doing God's will?

Your vote isn't just about politics—it's about faith. It's about showing the world who you really serve. Joshua put it perfectly: "Choose this day whom you will serve..." (Joshua 24:15).

The time for sitting on the fence is over.

The Rock That Never Moves

Every day, voices demand your attention. Politicians make promises. TV hosts try to convince you. Social media fills your head with a thousand different opinions. The Democratic Party offers its own tempting package: compassion, progress, justice for all.

But if you follow Jesus, there's only one voice that matters: God's Word.

The Bible Has the Final Say on Everything

It's not just another book written by people. It's God speaking directly to us. "All Scripture is breathed out by God and is useful for teaching, for reproof, for correction, and for training in righteousness, so that the man of God may be complete, equipped for every good work" (2 Timothy 3:16-17).

Notice those last three words: "every good work." Paul didn't say "some good works" or "church good works." He said every good work—and that includes voting.

Too many Christians treat the Bible like a Sunday-only book. They read it for personal comfort but ignore it when making real-world decisions. That's not how God designed it to work. As Psalm 138:2 says, God has put His Word above everything else—not just spiritual things, but everything.

When we vote based on what sounds good instead of what God says, we're putting human wisdom above God's wisdom, and that never ends well.

God's Word Covers Everything

The Bible isn't just for prayer time and church. It speaks clearly to every part of life, including how we vote. "I will never forget your precepts, for by them you have given me life" (Psalm 119:93).

Today's Democratic leaders often act like human thinking is more important than God's truth. But God's thoughts are higher than ours (Isaiah 55:8-9). When politicians say one thing and God says another, who are you going to trust?

Here's a simple test for any political platform: Does it protect innocent life? Does it promote real justice that matches God's character? Does it support God's design for families? The current Democratic agenda fails all these tests.

Voting is Worship

When you mark that ballot, you're declaring what you really believe. Ephesians 5:10 tells us to "try to discern what is pleasing to the Lord." That doesn't stop at the church door.

Democrats love to say, "Keep your faith out of politics." But that's not biblical. Faith isn't something you hide away when making important decisions. It's the lens you see everything through.

The Dangerous Middle Ground

Compromise sounds nice. It promises peace between two sides that can't both be right. Some Christians try to support the Democratic Party while keeping their faith, but it doesn't work. The tension tears them apart and weakens their witness.

Paul warns us: "Do not be deceived: Bad company corrupts good character" (1 Corinthians 15:33). This isn't just about the friends you hang out with. It's about the ideas you align yourself with.

Here's how compromise usually works: First, you tell yourself you can support the party while disagreeing on abortion. Then you start thinking maybe these issues aren't so clear after all. Finally, you convince yourself the Bible needs updating for modern times.

Jesus cuts through this self-deception: "If you abide in my word, you are truly my disciples, and you will know the truth, and the truth will set you free" (John 8:31-32). Real followers of Jesus don't pick and choose which parts of God's Word to obey.

The Democratic Party's history should warn us. They once supported slavery and segregation, choosing human wisdom over God's justice. Today they continue this pattern, deliberately leaving God out while supporting abortion and redefining marriage.

Even worse, some Democratic leaders twist Bible verses to support their agenda. Peter warned about this: "False teachers among you, who will secretly bring in destructive heresies" (2 Peter 2:1). Using God's Word to support what God opposes is dangerous territory.

When Christians water down Scripture's authority, they lose their ability to speak truth to culture. "When the righteous are in authority, the people rejoice; but when a wicked man rules, the people groan" (Proverbs 29:2).

How to Handle God's Word Right

If you want to stand strong, you need to handle the Bible correctly. Paul wrote: "Be diligent to present yourself approved to God, a worker who does not need to be ashamed, rightly dividing the word of truth" (2 Timothy 2:15).

Scripture isn't clay that you can mold to fit your politics. It's God's truth, unchanging and final. Reading it right means paying attention to context and avoiding the traps that lead to compromise.

Here's a common trick: Someone quotes "love your neighbor" to support same-sex marriage or open borders, making anyone who disagrees look unloving. But this ignores what the Bible says about love. First John 5:3 teaches: "For this is the love of God, that we keep his commandments." Real love works within God's design, not against it.

Be like the people in Berea, who "received the word with all readiness, and searched the Scriptures daily to find out whether these things were so" (Acts 17:11). When you know God's Word deeply, you can spot lies easily.

Handle Scripture as a whole, not in pieces. You can't champion one Bible truth while ignoring others. Jesus warned: "Whoever therefore breaks one of the least of these commandments, and teaches men so, shall be called least in the kingdom of heaven" (Matthew 5:19).

Standing on the Rock

In a world that twists truth and pressures you to compromise, Scripture stands firm. Ephesians 6:17 calls God's Word "the sword of the Spirit." For Christians facing the tempting promises of the Democratic Party, this sword is your best defense.

Scripture's power lies in showing truth and guiding decisions. The psalmist wrote: "Blessed are the undefiled in the way, who walk in the law of the Lord!" (Psalm 119:1). When you soak yourself in God's Word, you build a heart that resists sin and a mind that knows God's will.

Every vote you cast is a choice: Will you stand for Scripture's truth or give in to worldly thinking? As 2 Corinthians 5:20

reminds us we are ambassadors for Christ. Your political choices should show that you represent God's kingdom.

Standing on Scripture takes work. Psalm 1:2 describes the blessed person: "But his delight is in the law of the Lord, and in His law he meditates day and night." This kind of commitment turns voting into worship—a deliberate choice to align with God's kingdom rather than political promises.

The cost of compromise is huge. When Christians bend biblical truth, they weaken their witness and encourage ideas that lead to moral chaos. The Democratic Party's rejection of biblical values helps create a culture that treats abortion as normal, redefines families, and promotes unjust government.

Standing firm isn't easy, but Scripture promises God's faithfulness. Jesus said: "These things I have spoken to you, that in Me you may have peace. In the world you will have tribulation; but be of good cheer, I have overcome the world" (John 16:33) and Psalm 119:165 declares: "Great peace have those who love Your law, and nothing causes them to stumble."

The coming chapters will show exactly how the Democratic Party has turned away from biblical truth. The message is clear: anchor your heart in Scripture. Let it shape every decision, including how you vote.

Some will argue that supporting Democrats aligns with biblical calls to help the poor. But Scripture doesn't allow pick-and-choose obedience. Deuteronomy 5:32 commands: "Therefore you shall be careful to do as the Lord your God has commanded you; you shall not turn aside to the right hand or to the left."

In this battle for truth, Scripture is your greatest weapon. Let it be the foundation you stand on—solid, unmovable, and uncompromised. As you prepare to vote, test every platform against God's Word. Make sure your choices show your ultimate loyalty to Christ.

Stand firm. No compromise. Let your vote declare the glory of the God who speaks through His eternal Word.

And nowhere is this rebellion against God's Word more horrific than in their bloodthirsty defense of abortion—the slaughter of the most innocent among us.

Chapter 2: Abortion and the Sanctity of Life

Since Roe v. Wade fell, Democrats have become more rabid than ever. They're not just defending abortion anymore—they're celebrating it. They light up buildings in pink. They call it "reproductive freedom." They demand abortion up until birth, and sometimes even after.

60 million dead babies[9]. That's more than every American killed in every war we've ever fought, multiplied by 50. That's more than the populations of Canada and Australia combined.

And they want more blood. The Democratic Party's 2024 platform[18] demands unlimited "reproductive freedom," taxpayer-funded abortions, and no restrictions whatsoever—even for late-term procedures that end the lives of babies who could survive outside the womb.

Some of these procedures are so brutal they defy description. Partial-birth abortion involves delivering a living baby feet-first, then ending the child's life before completing the delivery.

Even worse, when babies survive abortion attempts and are born alive, some facilities simply refuse to provide life-saving medical care. Instead, they keep these newborns "comfortable" until they die—a practice that is nothing short of infanticide. Even many pro-choice Americans were horrified when they learned these details, leading Congress to ban partial-birth abortion in 2003 and require medical care for born-alive infants. Yet Democratic leaders opposed both bans and continue to fight any restrictions on late-term procedures.

As a Christian walking into that voting booth, you face a critical question: Can you follow Jesus and support a party that champions this?

The answer is clear: Life is sacred, and the Democratic Party stands against it.

Life as God's Sacred Gift

Every human life is not an accident—it is a masterpiece shaped by God's own hands. "I will praise You, for I am fearfully and wonderfully made; marvelous are Your works, and that my soul knows very well" (Psalm 139:14). This divine fingerprint marks every person—born and unborn alike.

The Bible makes this unmistakably clear. In Psalm 139:13-16, David declares: "For You formed my inward parts; You covered me in my mother's womb. I will praise You, for I am fearfully and wonderfully made... Your eyes saw my substance, being yet unformed. And in Your book they all were written, the days fashioned for me, when as yet there were none of them."

God doesn't start caring about us at birth—He's involved from the very beginning, forming us, knowing us, loving us. Jeremiah

1:5 confirms this: "Before I formed you in the womb I knew you; before you were born I sanctified you."

In contrast, the Democratic Party sees it differently. Their 2024 platform treats "reproductive freedom" as a fundamental right, supporting unlimited abortion access including procedures that end babies who could live outside the womb. They want to force you to pay for it with your tax dollars, making every American complicit in what Scripture clearly condemns.

Think about this: God says in Deuteronomy 27:25, "Cursed is the one who takes a bribe to slay an innocent person." Proverbs 6:16-17 makes it even clearer: among the things the Lord hates are "hands that shed innocent blood." When we choose abortion for convenience, economics, or personal choice, we place ourselves in direct opposition to God's own heart.

What About Rape and Incest?

When faced with the overwhelming evidence that abortion ends innocent human lives, those who claim the name of Christ but still vote democrat retreat to their final argument: "But what about rape and incest? Surely God wouldn't expect a woman to carry that baby."

This sounds compassionate. It feels reasonable. But here's the uncomfortable truth: Even this tragic exception doesn't justify supporting a party that champions abortions without limits at any time. Less than 1% of abortions are connected to rape or incest[7], yet that rare exception is used to defend abortion on demand for all nine months. Biblically, God never condones answering one act of evil with another. The violence of rape is not undone by the violence of abortion; it only multiplies the harm by destroying an innocent child. No tragedy, however heartbreaking, can ever make the murder of the innocent acceptable.

God's Heart for the Innocent

Even in heartbreaking circumstances, two wrongs don't make a right. The baby conceived in violence is still created in God's image. That child didn't commit the crime—why should they receive the death penalty?

Over and over again, history and personal testimonies confirm what Scripture already declares: every life has worth, even when the world says otherwise. Whether the pressure comes from violence, poverty, or medical predictions, God has proven that when life is chosen, blessings follow.

Consider the testimony of Juda Myers, who discovered she was conceived in rape. Her mother was brutally attacked, yet she chose life. Today Juda is a powerful pro-life advocate whose story has saved countless unborn children. She stands as living proof that God can bring beauty from ashes, purpose from pain.

Not all pressure comes from violence. Sometimes it comes from hardship, or the fear of hardship.

Maria Dolores, already a mother, was living in poverty and felt overwhelmed. She considered abortion and even sought it out. But when she asked, the doctor refused to perform the procedure. That "no" was more than a doctor's decision—it was God's intervention. She carried the pregnancy to term, and the child she once thought she could not raise became Cristiano Ronaldo—one of the greatest soccer athletes in history, admired worldwide for his talent, discipline, and determination. His story is a powerful reminder that even when fear says, *end it*,

God says, *this life matters*. Her story reminds us that hardship must never outweigh the value of life.

Other times pressure comes cloaked in medical authority—heavy, fearful, and persuasive.

Then, there is my own family's story. When my daughter was pregnant with her third child, doctors discovered a genetic marker—trisomy 21, associated with Down syndrome, along with signs of neural tube defects. From that moment forward, nearly every appointment came with pressure to terminate. The warnings grew darker: *"If the baby survives to term, she may be born with only part of her brain developed... she may be missing vital organs...she may have an open spine... she will suffer."*

One day, her husband was able to attend. When the doctor tried the same tactics on him, he stood firm: *"Whatever God gives us, God gives us."* His words stopped the pressure in its tracks.

We fasted, we prayed, and we trusted the Lord. God worked a miracle. My granddaughter was born physically perfect—not with the horrors doctors predicted. Today she thrives: an honor student, a soccer standout, a living testimony that every life is worth protecting.

After she was born, I asked my daughter how she could remain so strong under that pressure and never consider termination. Her answer floored me: *"Even if my baby had been born with severe defects, she could still be someone else's eyes... someone else's heart... someone else's liver. She could give life to another child. That was worth everything."* It was the greatest sacrificial love I have ever seen—a love that reflected the very heart of God.

These stories are not rare exceptions; they are reminders of a divine pattern. When life is preserved, God writes a story greater than fear, greater than pain, greater than human expectation. Each child spared is a testimony that His ways are higher, and His purposes will not be thwarted.

Isaiah 49:15-16 reveals God's heart: "Can a woman forget her nursing child, and not have compassion on the son of her womb? Surely they may forget, yet I will not forget you. See, I have inscribed you on the palms of My hands." God's love extends to every child, regardless of the circumstances of their conception.

God's heart is clear. He has always defended the weak and the innocent: "Deliver those who are drawn toward death, and hold back those stumbling to the slaughter" (Proverbs 24:11). The enemy, from the very beginning, has sought to destroy what is most precious to God. From Pharaoh killing Hebrew infants in Egypt, to Herod slaughtering babies in Bethlehem, Satan has always been after the children. Why? Because they are precious to God. Because their lives bear His image. Because their laughter and future bring Him glory. Jesus Himself declared, "Let the little children come to Me, and do not forbid them; for of such is the kingdom of God" (Mark 10:14).

The Real Question

But here's the reality: many who defend abortion argue for the rare cases of rape and incest, yet they support a political platform that pushes abortion for any reason, at any time.

The Democratic Party's platform is not about rare exceptions—it's about unrestricted abortion. Their 2024 platform demands:

- Abortion for any reason through all nine months
- Taxpayer funding for all abortions
- No parental consent for minors
- No waiting periods or counseling requirements
- No conscience protections for healthcare workers

So let's be clear: supporting this platform isn't about protecting the 1% in tragic circumstances. It's about endorsing the systematic elimination of millions of healthy babies whose only "crime" was being inconvenient.

The Ugly Truth About Abortion's Roots

Here's something the Democratic Party doesn't want you to know: modern abortion advocacy has roots in a movement designed to eliminate the "undesirable."

Margaret Sanger[8], founder of Planned Parenthood, openly wrote in 1921 that "the most urgent problem today" was how to stop "the mentally and physically defective" from reproducing. She specifically targeted the poor, the disabled, and minorities.

Today, Planned Parenthood performs nearly 40% of all U.S. abortions[5]—about 350,000 each year (making them the single largest provider). Their clinics are disproportionately located in Black and Hispanic neighborhoods. The result? Black women make up 14% of the female population, but account for 38% of abortions[6]. This isn't coincidence. It's a system designed to target the vulnerable, and it's still being funded with hundreds of millions of taxpayer dollars annually. Despite claims of funding cuts in recent years, Planned Parenthood continues to receive substantial taxpayer money, largely through Medicaid reimbursements and Title X family planning programs. While these funds are technically restricted from being used directly for abortion procedures, the reality is that money is interchangeable. By covering other expenses, taxpayer dollars free up Planned Parenthood's internal resources to continue providing abortions on a massive scale. In practice, this means Americans are still footing the bill for the nation's largest abortion provider.

This isn't just modern politics—it's an ancient evil in new clothes.

Ancient Evil, Modern Practice

In the Old Testament, parents sacrificed their children to false gods like Molech, burning them alive for prosperity and gain. God was outraged: "And you shall not let any of your descendants pass through the fire to Molech, nor shall you profane the name of your God: I am the Lord" (Leviticus 18:21).

Sound familiar? Today, children are sacrificed on the altar of personal choice. The methods have changed, but the heart is the same—innocent lives exchanged for adult convenience.

Jeremiah 7:31 records God's grief: "And they have built the high places of Tophet, which is in the Valley of the Son of Hinnom, to burn their sons and their daughters in the fire, which I did not command, nor did it come into My heart."

God never intended for children to be sacrificed for their parents' comfort. Yet that is exactly what abortion represents.

We must not miss the deeper spiritual reality at work: From Pharaoh's slaughter of Hebrew infants to Herod's massacre in Bethlehem, to the abortion industry today. Satan has always been after the children. The enemy targets what is most precious to God. Abortion is not only a political issue—it is spiritual warfare.

No Compromise on Sacred Ground

Jesus said, "Whoever receives one little child like this in My name receives Me" (Matthew 18:5). No exceptions.

Isaiah 1:15-17 warns, "When you spread out your hands, I will hide My eyes from you; even though you make many prayers, I will not hear. Your hands are full of blood. Wash yourselves, make yourselves clean; put away the evil of your doings from before My eyes. Cease to do evil, learn to do good; seek justice, rebuke the oppressor; defend the fatherless, plead for the widow."

To follow Christ while supporting policies that shed innocent blood is a contradiction that cannot stand.

It is God who opens the womb—period. Not just when the baby is wanted. Every life has purpose. Every heartbeat has meaning, and every child deserves the chance to fulfill the destiny God has planned for them.

The blood of the innocent cries out, and God hears every cry. But the Democratic assault on His creation doesn't end in the womb.

The same party that murders children before birth is determined to mutilate and confuse the ones who survive. They've moved from destroying bodies to destroying identities.

From attacking life itself to attacking the very image of God stamped on every human soul—male and female, exactly as He created them.

If you can stomach what they do to babies, wait until you see what they're doing to your children.

Chapter 3: Marriage, Sexuality, and Gender

"Mommy, why does my teacher call Jimmy 'she' now?"

That's the question millions of parents are facing as their children come home confused, disturbed, and indoctrinated. Five-year-olds are being taught they can choose their gender. Twelve-year-olds are being given puberty blockers. Teenage girls are having their breasts removed.

This is happening right now, in your schools, with your tax dollars, while Democrats cheer it on.

They champion same-sex marriage as a "right." They push transgender ideology on our children. They demand pronouns that deny biological reality. They are even targeting kids as young as 12 with irreversible medical procedures, often without parents knowing.

This isn't just politics. This is war against God's design for humanity.

As you prepare to vote, ask yourself: Can I follow Jesus and support a party that rejects everything He created regarding marriage, family, and gender?

The answer from Scripture is clear: **God's design is sacred, non-negotiable ground, and the Democratic Party has chosen to stand in open rebellion against it.**

God's Blueprint for Relationships

God didn't leave us guessing about relationships. He gave us a clear blueprint from the very beginning.

Genesis 5:2 tells us: "Male and female He created them, and He blessed them and called them Mankind in the day they were created." Notice that? Male and female. Not a spectrum, not fluid, not whatever you feel like today. Two distinct, complementary genders designed to work together.

Jesus made this even clearer in Mark 10:6-9: "But from the beginning of the creation, God 'made them male and female.' 'For this reason a man shall leave his father and mother and be joined to his wife, and the two shall become one flesh'; so then they are no longer two, but one flesh. Therefore what God has joined together, let not man separate."

Jesus pointed back to the beginning—God's original design. One man, one woman, joined together for life. This isn't just a nice idea or an outdated tradition. It's God's sacred pattern for human relationships.

The Democratic Party's 2024 platform treats this as discrimination. They celebrate same-sex marriage as a fundamental right, building on court decisions that redefined marriage against thousands of years of human history. They push transgender policies that let people ignore their biological reality and demand that everyone else play along.

At its core, marriage cannot be redefined by man. It is more than a legal contract or personal preference; it is a divine covenant established by God Himself.

It isn't just about two people who love each other; it reflects a relationship so sacred that changing its definition attacks the very image of God.

Paul emphasized this same truth when he wrote to the Ephesians, reminding them that marriage reflects the mystery of Christ and His church.

What Scripture Actually Says About Homosexuality

A 2023 poll revealed that 71% of Americans now view homosexuality as morally acceptable[1]—a dramatic shift driven largely by Democratic advocacy over the past thirty years. The Democratic Party openly celebrates what Scripture calls sin, encouraging people to embrace identities that lead to spiritual death. Even more concerning, surveys show that 55% of self-identified Christians now affirm same-sex marriage as acceptable[2], reflecting how deeply cultural slogans like "love is love" have influenced the Church.

Yet the Bible does not whisper about this issue; it speaks with clarity. Leviticus 18:22 declares: "You shall not lie with a male as with a woman. It is an abomination." Romans 1:26-27 adds: "For this reason God gave them up to vile passions. For even their women exchanged the natural use for what is against nature. Likewise also the men, leaving the natural use of the woman, burned in their lust for one another, men with men committing what is shameful, and receiving in themselves the penalty of their error which was due."

Scripture's teaching leaves no ambiguity—homosexual behavior is sin. But it's important to remember that this sin is not isolated or unique. Paul's letters list many sins—idolatry, greed, adultery, drunkenness—right alongside homosexuality. The point is not to single one out as if it were unforgivable, but to show that all of us stand guilty before a holy God and in need of His mercy.

And this is where the gospel shines. Christianity is not just about rules; it's about redemption. First Corinthians 6:11 reminds us: "And such were some of you. But you were washed, but you were sanctified, but you were justified in the name of the Lord Jesus and by the Spirit of our God."

The key phrase is "such were some of you." Past tense. Through Christ, anyone—no matter their past—can be washed, sanctified, and made new. God's grace can transform anyone who turns to Him.

The Attack on God's Design for Gender

Deuteronomy 22:5 declares: "A woman shall not wear anything that pertains to a man, nor shall a man put on a woman's garment, for all who do so are an abomination to the Lord your God."

This passage is often misunderstood. It is not primarily about whether women can wear pants—when the law was given, pants as we know them did not even exist. The command goes far deeper. It warns against the deliberate erasing of the God-given distinction between male and female. This is not a matter of fabric, but of identity. To put on the appearance or role of the opposite sex is to deny God's created order.

From the beginning, God created humanity in His image, declaring, "male and female He created them" (Genesis 1:27). These distinctions were purposeful, reflecting both the complementarity of men and women and the covenant picture of Christ and His Church. When Moses calls cross-dressing an "abomination," the reason is not cultural preference, but because such actions attempt to undo God's very design.

Today, this truth collides with one of the most aggressive ideologies of our time: transgenderism. Our culture insists gender is a modern ideology, a social construct, fluid and self-determined. But Scripture testifies that gender is not self-created—it is God-ordained. To claim the authority to redefine it is to usurp the Creator Himself.

The transgender movement does not merely confuse clothing styles; it redefines identity itself. It says a man can declare himself a woman, and society must affirm the lie. It elevates subjective feelings above biological reality, demanding that truth bend to personal preference. Yet this deception does not bring freedom—it brings bondage, leaving countless lives broken and scarred.

And the consequences are not just personal—they are cultural. When men are allowed to compete in women's sports, decades of hard-won opportunities for women are erased in the name of "inclusion." When biological men are permitted in women's restrooms and locker rooms, women and girls lose privacy and safety. When children are taught that they can change their gender at will, they are robbed of stability and truth at the most formative stages of life.

Even more grievous is the rise of so-called "gender-affirming care," which is nothing less than child mutilation. Minors are being subjected to puberty blockers, cross-sex hormones, and irreversible surgeries that leave them sterile, scarred, and broken. Many times, this is even done without the knowledge or consent of their parents. These children cannot legally buy alcohol, vote, or even get a tattoo—yet our culture allows them to make life-altering decisions that destroy their God-given bodies. This is not compassion; it is cruelty masquerading as progress.

Christians must not minimize this. The rejection of male and female as fixed realities is not a minor issue of personal choice; it is open rebellion against the order of creation. It is an attack on the image of God in humanity, and a distortion of the gospel picture God embedded in marriage and family.

The Pronoun Delusion

"Woe to those who call evil good, and good evil; who put darkness for light, and light for darkness; who put bitter for sweet, and sweet for bitter!" (Isaiah 5:20). That is exactly what is happening in America today. Our culture has traded the unshakable truth of God's creation for man-made lies—and nowhere is this more obvious than in the pronoun delusion.

This battle is not about grammar; it is about reality. God created us male and female, distinct and purposeful, reflecting His design. "So God created man in His own image; in the image of God He created him; male and female He created them" (Genesis 1:27). But the modern world insists otherwise. A man can demand to be called "she." A woman can insist on "he" or even "they," as if one person could somehow be plural. Activists have gone further, inventing an ever-expanding list of so-called "neo-pronouns"—more than 70 in circulation today—including words like "ze," "hir," and "xe." Some even claim animal identities, demanding recognition as cats, wolves, or other fantasies, insisting society must comply.

But let's be honest—this is not progress. It is confusion, and in many cases, it is mental illness. If someone believes they are a cat or insists that reality bends to their self-identification, they are not in touch with truth. And when Christians "play along" by affirming these delusions with false pronouns, we are not showing kindness—we are enabling brokenness. Scripture is clear: "Lying lips are an abomination to the Lord, but those who deal truthfully are His delight" (Proverbs 12:22). To affirm lies in the name of compassion is to sin against truth. True love does not indulge mental illness; true love speaks truth, even when it is costly.

And here is where the political line becomes undeniable. The Democratic Party has not only embraced the pronoun delusion—they are enforcing it. Their 2024 platform elevates "gender identity" as equal to biological sex and demands that government, schools, and workplaces require the use of preferred pronouns. Teachers have been suspended or fired for refusing to participate in the lie. Businesses face lawsuits if employees "misgender" someone. Children are indoctrinated in taxpayer-funded schools, told that rejecting these false pronouns is hateful, while parents are sidelined.

This is not freedom—it is forced compliance. The Democratic Party insists that everyone must participate in the delusion, even if it means violating conscience, Scripture, or basic truth itself. By demanding that Christians speak what they know to be false, they are asking us to exchange the truth of God for a lie.

The pronoun issue may appear small compared to larger cultural battles, but it strikes at the very foundation of truth. If words can be redefined, then reality itself can be reshaped by ideology. And when reality is surrendered to lies, the door is opened to every form of deception. This is why Christians cannot compromise here. To embrace the Democratic Party's agenda is to endorse a worldview that denies truth itself—and ultimately denies the God who is Truth.

The Slippery Slope Is Real

When a society rejects God's design in one area, it will not stop there. Once you open the door to redefining marriage, sexuality, or gender, there are no guardrails left. One compromise becomes the justification for the next, and before long, truth itself is up for grabs.

This is exactly what we see unfolding in America. First, marriage was redefined from God's covenant between one man and one woman into a political "right" that could mean anything. Then, sexuality itself was redefined—not as a sacred gift to be expressed within God's boundaries, but as an identity to be celebrated regardless of whether it aligned with His Word. Now, gender is being redefined—not as a biological reality, but as a fluid choice, subject to feelings and personal preference.

The result? A culture where truth is exchanged for lies. Romans 1:25 warns us: "who exchanged the truth of God for the lie, and worshiped and served the creature rather than the Creator, who is blessed forever. Amen." This is the spiritual progression of rebellion: deny God's authority, redefine His creation, and eventually worship human feelings above His truth.

This is not a harmless social trend. It is a moral landslide. Today, we hear absurd claims like "you can be whatever you identify as"—even if that means calling yourself a cat or dozens of newly invented pronouns that deny reality. What was once unthinkable is now celebrated. What was once considered mental illness is now normalized, even demanded. And every step down this slope takes our culture further from God and deeper into bondage.

The Democratic Party is not just a passive observer of this decline; they are leading the charge. They enshrine these lies in policy, push them into schools, and punish those who dare to dissent. The slippery slope is not hypothetical—it's happening right now, and Christians cannot close their eyes to it.

As believers, we must recognize that this is not about politics alone. It is about whether we will stand with God's unchanging truth or go along with a culture sliding into darkness. If we compromise here, there will be no bottom to this slope.

What's at Stake for Christians and the Church

The slippery slope we see in culture is not just "out there." It directly impacts the people of God. If the Church compromises or stays silent, the decline will not stop at the edges of society— it will sweep right into the body of Christ.

We are already seeing it. Polls show that a majority of self-identified Christians now affirm same-sex marriage. Entire denominations have embraced LGBTQ ideology, blessing unions that Scripture calls sin, ordaining leaders who reject

God's design, and teaching young people that the Bible is outdated or irrelevant. When the Church echoes the world instead of God's Word, it loses its prophetic voice. Salt loses its saltiness. Light is hidden under a basket.

Jesus warned of this in Matthew 5:13-14: "You are the salt of the earth; but if the salt loses its flavor, how shall it be seasoned? It is then good for nothing but to be thrown out and trampled underfoot by men. You are the light of the world. A city that is set on a hill cannot be hidden." If we fail to stand for truth, the culture will trample what remains of Christian witness.

What's at stake is not only public policy but also the spiritual health of the Church. The Democratic Party's platform doesn't just pressure government—it pressures Christians to conform, to keep quiet, and to bless what God condemns. And too many churches are caving under that pressure.

This is why silence is not an option. When lies about marriage, sexuality, and gender take root, they destroy families, confuse children, and corrupt the witness of the Church. But when God's people stand firm on His Word, even when it's unpopular, they offer hope and clarity to a world drowning in confusion.

The question for the Church today is simple: Will we stand with the Creator, or will we bow to the culture? Will we remain faithful to God's design, or will we exchange truth for lies? The stakes could not be higher.

The Church's Moment of Truth

The slippery slope isn't just out there in the culture—it has crept into the pews. The American church in many ways has become weak, afraid to preach on sin, terrified of being labeled "hateful" or "intolerant." Instead of being salt and light, too many pastors have traded courage for comfort and truth for applause.

We see entire denominations rewriting their statements on marriage. We see pulpits where the Bible is no longer proclaimed with boldness, but where sermons are shaped to avoid offense. We see churches waving rainbow flags, celebrating what God calls an abomination, all in the name of "love." We even see churches that don't open Bibles at all anymore, where the Word of God is replaced with motivational speeches and cultural clichés.

And then there are pastors who preach messages like "10 steps to get all you can out of God," treating Him as if He were some genie granting wishes, rather than the holy and sovereign King who calls us to repentance. They tickle ears, but they don't pierce hearts. They give people tips for a better life, but not the truth that leads to eternal life.

This is the moment of truth. Will the church stand with the world, or will it stand with Christ? Jesus never softened the truth to avoid offending the crowd. The apostles never watered down the gospel to gain political favor. The call of the church has always been clear: "Preach the word! Be ready in season and out of season. Convince, rebuke, exhort, with all longsuffering and teaching" (2 Timothy 4:2).

And here is where the choice becomes unmistakable. The Democratic Party does not merely drift from biblical truth—it stands in open rebellion against it. To align with that platform is to align with policies that bless what God curses, celebrate what God condemns, and promote confusion where God has spoken with clarity. A church that refuses to speak against sin, or worse, aligns itself with the very party pushing these deceptions, is no longer standing with Christ but with the world.

The modern American church is at a crossroads. Silence in the face of sin is not compassion—it is complicity. Fear of man has replaced fear of God, and if the church does not wake up, it will find itself standing shoulder to shoulder with the world in open rebellion against its Creator. As David declared: "In God I have put my trust; I will not fear. What can flesh do to me?" (Psalm 56:11).

This is why no Christian can, with a clear conscience, cast their vote for the Democratic Party.

But the moral compromises don't stop with marriage and gender. The same party that perverts God's design for humanity has also perverted His design for work, prosperity, and provision. They've replaced biblical stewardship with government slavery.

Chapter 4: Economic Policies and Biblical Stewardship

Look at the homeless camps spreading like cancer through every Democrat-run city. San Francisco's streets reek of human waste while tech billionaires step over bodies on their way to work. Los Angeles burns through billions in "homeless initiatives" while tent cities multiply like a plague. Seattle watches businesses flee as addicts shoot up in broad daylight.

This is the fruit of Democratic economics: dependency, despair, and death.

They promised compassion. They delivered hell.

God designed work to give us dignity, purpose, and the ability to provide for our families. But Democrats have built an empire of welfare slavery that strips people of all three. They've replaced the satisfaction of an honest day's work with the degradation of government handouts. They've traded human dignity for votes.

And they call this progress.

God's Call to Faithful Stewardship

From the very beginning, God made us to work, to create, to build.

"Then the Lord God took the man and put him in the garden of Eden to tend and keep it" (Genesis 2:15).

Work wasn't punishment—it was paradise. Adam didn't sit around collecting heavenly welfare checks. He worked. He cultivated. He took raw creation and made it flourish. That's what we were designed for.

Look at Joseph in Genesis. When famine threatened to destroy Egypt, he didn't create food stamps and universal basic income. He worked. He planned. He stored grain during seven years of plenty to prepare for seven years of famine. His wisdom and hard work saved entire nations from starvation (Genesis 41:46-57).

Joseph's stewardship is God's model: Work while you can. Save what you earn. Prepare for hard times. Take responsibility for yourself and help others from your abundance.

Now look at the Democratic model: Spend what you don't have. Borrow from China. Print money until it's worthless. Make people dependent on government checks so they'll never dare vote against you. It's not stewardship—it's sabotage.

Jesus drove this home in the Parable of the Talents (Matthew 25:14-30). The master gave his servants money and expected them to multiply it through work and wise investment. Those who worked and produced were rewarded. The lazy servant who buried his talent? He was cast into outer darkness.

Let that sink in: Jesus literally said the lazy servant deserved hell.

But Democrats reward laziness and punish productivity. They take from those who work and give to those who won't. They've inverted Christ's parable and wonder why our cities are collapsing.

Work: God's Blueprint for Human Flourishing

Scripture doesn't whisper about work—it shouts.

"For even when we were with you, we commanded you this: If anyone will not work, neither shall he eat" (2 Thessalonians 3:10).

Paul didn't stutter. No work, no food. It's that simple. But Democrats have created a system where you can collect more money sitting at home than breaking your back at a job. They've made work optional and welfare optimal.

Drive through any inner city that Democrats have controlled for decades. What do you see? Able-bodied men standing on corners at 2 PM on a Tuesday. Three generations of families who've never held a job. Teenagers who've never seen their parents go to work. This isn't compassion—it's calculated cruelty.

"The hand of the diligent will rule, but the lazy man will be put to forced labor" (Proverbs 10:4).

But Democrats have severed the link between diligence and prosperity. They've told people that poverty is someone else's fault. That success is "privilege." That work is oppression. They've lied to millions, and those lies have destroyed entire communities.

I've seen it firsthand. Good neighborhoods turned into war zones. Families that once thrived now trapped in generational poverty. Young men who should be learning trades are instead learning how to game the welfare system. Young women having babies for bigger government checks, raising fatherless children who'll repeat the cycle.

This is what Democratic economics produces: hopelessness manufactured by government design.

Real Charity vs. Forced Redistribution

Here's what burns me up: Democrats hide their theft behind the word "compassion."

God commands us to be generous. "So let each one give as he purposes in his heart, not grudgingly or of necessity; for God loves a cheerful giver" (2 Corinthians 9:7).

See those words? "Not of necessity." God wants us to give from our hearts, not have it ripped from our paychecks by politicians buying votes with our money.

When the Good Samaritan found a beaten man on the road (Luke 10:25-37), he didn't petition Rome for a new tax. He reached into his own pocket. He paid from his own wealth. That's real charity—personal, sacrificial, voluntary.

But Democrats don't practice charity. They practice theft. They take from workers at gunpoint (try not paying your taxes and see what happens) and give it to people who vote for them. It's not compassion—it's a protection racket dressed up in moral language.

Even worse, their forced redistribution destroys real charity. Why should I help my neighbor when the government takes half my paycheck to supposedly do it for me? Why should churches feed the poor when food stamps exist? Why should communities care for their own when Uncle Sam will do it?

They've replaced love with legislation, community with government programs, and personal responsibility with perpetual dependence.

I know a man who runs a small construction company. He wanted to hire some young men from the neighborhood, teach them a trade, give them a future. But they all turned him down. Why? Because they'd lose their benefits. They could make more doing nothing than learning skills that would set them free.

That's the Democrat economy: where work is punished and laziness is paid.

The Weight of Debt and the Sin of Irresponsibility

Let me tell you what intergenerational theft looks like: $34 trillion in national debt[3].

Your children, your grandchildren, your great-grandchildren—they're already slaves to debt they didn't create. Democrats spent their futures before they were even born.

"The rich rules over the poor, and the borrower is servant to the lender" (Proverbs 22:7).

We're slaves to China. We're slaves to international bankers. We're slaves to anyone willing to buy our worthless treasury bonds. And Democrats keep spending like drunken sailors on shore leave.

They'll blow a trillion dollars on "infrastructure" that never gets built. They'll forgive student loans for gender studies majors while plumbers pay their bills. They'll send billions to Ukraine while East Palestine, Ohio, drinks poisoned water.

This isn't incompetence. It's intentional. Every dollar of debt is another chain around America's neck. Every welfare program is another family destroyed. Every handout is another soul sold for political power.

My grandfather worked 16-hour days in a steel mill to feed his family. He never took a dime he didn't earn. He'd be sick to see what we've become—a nation of beggars and thieves, ruled by politicians who've never done an honest day's work in their lives.

The Prosperity Gospel of Government

Here's the ultimate blasphemy: Democrats have replaced God with government.

They promise what only God can deliver—security, provision, purpose. They've become the false prophets Isaiah warned about, telling people to trust in princes instead of the Lord.

"Thus says the Lord: 'Cursed is the man who trusts in man and makes flesh his strength, whose heart departs from the Lord'" (Jeremiah 17:5).

Every government check is a counterfeit blessing. Every welfare program is a false gospel. Every promise of free money is a lie from the pit of hell.

You want to see what trusting in government instead of God produces? Look at Detroit—once the jewel of American industry, now a wasteland. Look at Baltimore, Chicago, St. Louis—all ruled by Democrats for generations, all dying from spiritual and economic cancer.

The government that promises to be your provider will become your master. The party that promises to care for you cradle to grave is building both your cradle and your grave.

Breaking Free from Economic Slavery

God's economic plan is simple: Work hard. Save money. Give generously. Take care of your family. Help your neighbor.

The Democratic economic plan: Don't work. Demand money. Take constantly. Abandon your family. Make your neighbor pay for your life.

These visions are absolutely incompatible. You cannot serve both God's design for human flourishing and the Democratic design for human dependency.

"Also that every man should eat and drink and enjoy the good of all his labor—it is the gift of God" (Ecclesiastes 3:13).

But Democrats say, "If anyone is not willing to work, give him food stamps, section 8 housing, free healthcare, and a monthly check."

You cannot reconcile these worldviews. One builds character; the other destroys it. One creates prosperity; the other creates poverty. One honors God; the other mocks Him.

The Christian Choice

I'll make this brutally simple: Every vote for a Democrat is a vote for theft, dependency, and the destruction of human dignity.

It's a vote to steal from workers to buy the loyalty of non-workers.

It's a vote to enslave your children to debt they can never repay.

It's a vote to replace God's design with government's dysfunction.

Jesus said you cannot serve both God and money (Matthew 6:24). Democrats have chosen money—specifically, your money, taken by force and used to buy power.

When you stand in that voting booth, you're not just choosing economic policy. You're choosing whether America will follow God's blueprint for prosperity or continue down the Democrat path to economic hell.

The tent cities are growing. The debt is exploding. The dependency is deepening. And Democrats want more—more spending, more welfare, more control, more souls sold for government checks.

Your vote will either feed this beast or starve it.

Choose wisely. Your children's futures depend on it.

Chapter 5: Religious Liberty and Free Speech

Jack Phillips just wanted to bake cakes. But when he politely declined to create a wedding cake celebrating what God calls sin, Democrats destroyed his life. Seven years of lawsuits. Death threats. Vandalism. Financial ruin.

His crime? Following his conscience.

This is Democrat America: where you're free to believe whatever you want—as long as you never act on it.

The modern Democrat agenda works to push God out of the public square and to punish those who will not bend their convictions to the culture. From scrubbing faith from civic life to coercing Christians in courtrooms and classrooms, the message is unmistakable: be quiet, conform, or be crushed.

This is not merely political theater. This is about your God-given right to worship Him and to speak His truth with a clear conscience.

God's Call to Worship and Witness

God does not whisper about worship and witness. He commands it.

"Declare His glory among the nations, His wonders among all peoples" (Psalm 96:3). That is not a private suggestion; it is a public summons. Christian speech is not a hobby for weekends. It is obedience.

When states or school boards attempt to mute Christian confession, the believer's duty does not change. "But as we have been approved by God to be entrusted with the gospel, even so we speak, not as pleasing men, but God who tests our hearts" (1 Thessalonians 2:4). The standard is clear: speak to please God.

Democrats prefer a faith that stays indoors and out of sight. God commands a faith that steps into the daylight and speaks.

Erasing God from Public Life

The Democrat project has a pattern: rewrite the rules so God's name disappears from the places where Americans gather and govern. Lawsuits to strip crosses from memorials, campaigns to remove Scripture from displays, pressure to replace "faith" with "neutrality" whenever the public square is in view. The strategy is subtraction: subtract symbols, subtract speech, subtract Scripture.

Scripture saw this spirit long ago. "Why do the nations rage, and the people plot a vain thing? The kings of the earth set themselves, and the rulers take counsel together, against the Lord and against His Anointed, saying, 'Let us break Their bonds in pieces and cast away Their cords from us'" (Psalm 2:1-

3). The desire is the same: cast off God's cords, call His truth a chain, and declare autonomy as freedom.

True freedom is different. "Stand fast therefore in the liberty by which Christ has made us free, and do not be entangled again with a yoke of bondage" (Galatians 5:1). When a party treats public acknowledgment of God as a problem to be solved, it does not liberate citizens; it binds them to speech codes where reverence is forbidden and rebellion is applauded.

Silencing Biblical Truth

Coercion now masquerades as "civil rights." Designers and bakers are hauled into court for refusing to celebrate what God calls sin. Teachers are threatened, disciplined, or dismissed for refusing to speak falsehood about male and female. Business owners are told they must create messages that violate conscience or be crushed by the state.

This is not neutrality; it is forced speech. God's standard is the opposite: "For we can do nothing against the truth, but for the truth" (2 Corinthians 13:8). When the state commands lies, Christians may not comply.

Democrats market this as "inclusion." The reality is compulsion. Policies that mandate preferred pronouns, require creative endorsement of same-sex unions, or punish dissenting speech do not protect the vulnerable; they punish the faithful. "The fear of man brings a snare, but whoever trusts in the Lord shall be safe" (Proverbs 29:25). The snare is set when the government demands assent to falsehood and calls it love.

Digital Censorship of Christians

A new gatekeeper emerged in our era: the algorithm. Posts quoting Scripture on marriage or gender disappear. Accounts are throttled, shadow-banned, or locked. Entire ministries find their reach mysteriously shrunk the moment biblical clarity appears in a caption.

God's answer is not retreat. "Forever, O Lord, Your word is settled in heaven" (Psalm 119:89). Platforms rise and fall; the Word remains. The right response is courage, not self-censorship. "The wicked flee when no one pursues, but the righteous are bold as a lion" (Proverbs 28:1).

I have lived this personally. Posts that quoted the Bible or challenged the cultural line were flagged. "Community standards" became the pretext for silencing biblical standards. Suspension and shadow-bans do not change the truth. They only expose who fears it.

The "Tolerance" Trap

Democrats sell "tolerance" while enshrining intolerance toward biblical conviction. The bargain is familiar: you may keep your faith if you never speak it, never appeal to it, and never let it shape your public actions. That is not tolerance; it is a gag order.

Paul asked a question that fits our moment: "Have I therefore become your enemy because I tell you the truth?" (Galatians 4:16). In a culture that equates affirmation with love, telling the truth will be labeled hate. The Christian answer is settled: love tells the truth or it is not love at all.

God's Word does not need cultural permission slips. "But sanctify the Lord God in your hearts, and always be ready to give a defense to everyone who asks you a reason for the hope that is in you, with meekness and fear" (1 Peter 3:15). Fear God, not the focus group.

What's Really at Stake

This is not a fight about slogans. This is about the gospel's public witness. "For I am not ashamed of the gospel of Christ, for it is the power of God to salvation for everyone who believes" (Romans 1:16). If Christians grow ashamed, the gospel grows silent in the very places it is most needed.

Christ set the standard for public allegiance: "For whoever is ashamed of Me and My words in this adulterous and sinful generation, of him the Son of Man also will be ashamed when He comes in the glory of His Father with the holy angels" (Mark 8:38). The cost of cultural comfort is too high. Better to be scorned by men than to be silent before God.

The Church's Fighting Spirit

History does not belong to the timid. The church has always advanced when ordinary believers chose courage over comfort. "I have fought the good fight, I have finished the race, I have kept the faith" (2 Timothy 4:7). That is the posture of faithful people in hostile times.

Our task is unchanged: preach the Word, gather without apology, and refuse to outsource conscience to the state. "Now the just shall live by faith; but if anyone draws back, My soul has no pleasure in him. But we are not of those who draw back to perdition, but of those who believe to the saving of the soul" (Hebrews 10:38-39). Shrinking back is not an option.

Voting for Freedom

Votes are not neutral. Votes choose a moral frame for the nation. Policies that muzzle biblical expression, penalize conscience, and scrub God from public life are not accidents; they are the fruit of a platform. Christians must vote accordingly.

Scripture names the effect plainly: "The wicked shall be turned into hell, and all the nations that forget God" (Psalm 9:17). If the people are groaning under speech codes and conscience coercion, it is time to change who governs.

Support candidates committed to protecting religious liberty in schools, businesses, and public service; defending free speech including biblical expression; preserving space for religious symbols and speech in the public square; and resisting censorship by proxies in Big Tech and bureaucracies.

Standing Without Compromise

This moment demands steel in the spine and tenderness in the heart. The church must be unflinching in truth and unafraid in love. "And do not be afraid of their threats, nor be troubled. But sanctify the Lord God in your hearts" (1 Peter 3:14-15). Courage is a witness.

Resolve this now: no more apologizing for Scripture, no more delegating conscience to the state, no more treating worship as negotiable. Faithful Christians will stand, speak, and suffer if needed. The promise is worth it. "Be faithful until death, and I will give you the crown of life" (Revelation 2:10).

You cannot serve both God and a party platform that punishes His people for telling the truth. Choose the side that guards the church's voice, protects the believer's conscience, and honors the Lord in public. Choose freedom. Choose faithfulness. Choose without compromise.

But nothing exposed the Democratic war on faith quite like COVID. What started as "two weeks to flatten the curve" became the greatest assault on religious liberty in American history. Churches were labeled "non-essential" while liquor stores stayed open. And most Americans—including most Christians—complied.

PM Kimbler

Chapter 6: COVID-19

This will be a long section—because what we lived through during COVID was not a small bump in history. It was a seismic turning point. COVID wasn't just a pandemic; it was a social experiment, a massive test of obedience, and the sad truth is that the majority of people complied without question.

From the beginning, the narrative was built on fear, and fear is the opposite of faith. Instead of turning to God, millions turned to government. Instead of trusting Scripture, they trusted "science" that changed by the week. Instead of standing firm on biblical conviction, churches and Christians caved to worldly pressure.

Every step of the crisis revealed something far darker than a public health emergency. It exposed a deliberate, anti-God, anti-biblical agenda. And let's be clear: the Democrat Party was at the tip of the spear. These were the people who seized on COVID to expand their power, strip away freedom, silence the church, and train Americans to obey without resistance.

This wasn't just a virus. It was a spiritual war. And as we walk back through it step by step, the pattern will become undeniable: biblical obedience to God was pitted against blind obedience to government—and the majority chose wrongly.

Lockdowns and Mask Mandates

We were told it would be "two weeks to flatten the curve." That was the slogan, the sales pitch, the bait. Two weeks turned into two years of tyranny. Democrats sold fear like snake oil, and Americans paid the price with their freedoms, their livelihoods, and their faith.

Businesses shuttered. Churches padlocked. Families cut off. Elderly people died alone in nursing homes. Funerals were forbidden, weddings postponed, and children kept from their grandparents. Meanwhile, the same politicians who demanded obedience broke their own rules, proving it was never about health—it was about control.

Hypocrisy in Action

California's Gavin Newsom banned church gatherings, forbade singing, and even outlawed home Bible studies. Yet liquor stores, pot shops, and abortion clinics were labeled "essential." Then he snuck off to the French Laundry restaurant for a lavish, maskless dinner with his friends.

In New York, Andrew Cuomo capped church gatherings at ten people while grocery stores, bars, and subway cars overflowed. Worse still, his order forcing COVID-positive patients into nursing homes killed thousands of vulnerable seniors. That blood is on his hands.

Michigan's Gretchen Whitmer banned churches while keeping abortion clinics wide open. She restricted families from buying seeds to plant gardens, while Planned Parenthood operated without interruption. Her policies were not science—they were anti-God.

And Nancy Pelosi? She paraded on TV about lockdown compliance, then got caught maskless in a San Francisco salon. The rules were never for them; they were only for us.

This wasn't a few bad politicians. This was the Democrat Party in lockstep, weaponizing a virus to grab power and choke out freedom.

Crushing the People

While elites enjoyed fine dining and secret privileges, everyday Americans paid the price. Small businesses—the backbone of the nation—were gutted. Restaurants, gyms, and family shops that survived generations collapsed overnight under government orders. "Non-essential," they said. Non-essential to who? Certainly not to the families who relied on them for survival. Meanwhile, Amazon, Walmart, and corporate giants thrived like never before.

Hospitals claimed to be overrun, yet nurses and doctors had time to choreograph TikTok dances in empty hallways. The same people who said funerals couldn't be held were posting videos mocking the very fear they helped create. That was not compassion—it was cruelty.

Children were robbed of childhood. Schools shut down, and classrooms moved to screens. Kids sat masked inside taped-off squares, their playgrounds wrapped in yellow police tape. Band students played instruments sealed inside plastic bubbles.

Proms were erased, graduations canceled, and academic progress fell off a cliff. Even worse, depression, anxiety, and teen suicide soared to record highs. Childhood itself was sacrificed on the altar of government control.

Behind closed doors, suffering multiplied. Lockdowns trapped women and children with abusive partners. Alcohol sales spiked, drug overdoses surged, and calls to suicide hotlines skyrocketed. Mental health was dismissed because obedience to government was more important to Democrats than compassion for people.

The Mask Charade

Masks became the symbol of submission. First, officials told us they were useless. Then they became mandatory. Then came the absurdity of double-masking. The rules shifted every week, and those who questioned it were shamed, silenced, or punished. Children were treated like criminals for pulling masks below their noses. Society lived in fear of a flimsy piece of cloth that never stopped a virus—but did succeed in dividing neighbor against neighbor.

Obedience, Not Safety

Lockdowns and mask mandates were never about saving lives. They were about testing compliance. How far would Americans bend? How quickly would they surrender their freedom? Sadly, the majority complied. That was the real experiment—not medicine, not science, but obedience.

They told us it was about saving lives, but it was always about control. The truth is plain: this was a social experiment, and the majority complied. The real question is not whether it happened—we lived it. The real question is what we, as Christians and as the church, will do next time.

Because when the pressure came, it wasn't just politicians who failed us. Many of the very shepherds who were supposed to lead God's people caved without a fight.

If the hypocrisy of the politicians was bad, the cowardice of the pastors was worse. While Democrats mocked God openly, the majority of pastors folded without a fight. Men who were called to shepherd with courage became mouthpieces for government edicts instead of heralds of the gospel.

When lockdowns came, the majority of churches went dark overnight. Most pastors hid behind Romans 13 as their excuse, telling their congregations that "obedience to government" mattered more than obedience to God. They locked their doors, silenced worship, and claimed that a livestream was good enough.

The truth is simple: church is not a Netflix show. Yet most pastors trained their flocks to stay home in pajamas, sip coffee, and "watch church" like it was just another program. Hebrews 10:25 commands believers not to forsake "the assembling of ourselves together," but cowardly leadership taught people that convenience was more important than conviction. The scar left on the American church is permanent. Attendance has never recovered, and many now believe gathering in person is optional. That didn't happen by accident. It happened because the majority of pastors surrendered.

Joel Osteen, the smiling prosperity salesman of Houston, locked his building but kept his money machine running. His people were fleeced while he refused to shepherd them. T.D.

Jakes, another prosperity empire-builder, not only closed his doors but went further—pushing Caesar's syringe on his flock, promoting the vaccine as though it were salvation itself. Their allegiance was not to Christ or Scripture. It was to cash, influence, and government approval.

The tragedy is that they were not alone. From small-town pulpits to massive megachurches, most pastors folded without resistance. They bowed to fear, bent to government, and betrayed the God they claimed to serve.

Yet there were exceptions. A handful of pastors stood firm. They risked fines, arrest, and even prison to keep their doors open and their people fed. While the majority compromised, these few proved what real faith looks like. Their courage shines all the brighter against the backdrop of so much cowardice.

While most pastors cowered behind closed doors, a remnant stood like warriors on the battlefield. They didn't bend, they didn't bow, and they refused to let the government dictate the mission of Christ's church.

John MacArthur was one of them. In the heart of California's tyranny, when politicians declared church "non-essential," he thundered back with action. He flung open the doors of Grace Community Church and told the government to get out of Christ's way. Fines, lawsuits, and threats rained down, but MacArthur stood firm. And when the smoke cleared, the state that tried to silence him was forced to pay. He didn't just win for his church—he struck a blow for religious liberty in America.

Standing with the same fire was Jack Hibbs of Calvary Chapel Chino Hills. From day one, Hibbs refused to let his pulpit go dark. His church became a lighthouse in the storm—filled week after week while others shut down and hid. Thousands gathered, not in defiance of government, but in obedience to God. Hibbs declared boldly that worship is not optional, it is essential, and no politician has the authority to tell God's people otherwise.

And they were not alone. Across America, other faithful pastors showed the same grit. They faced fines, harassment, and threats, yet they never flinched. Their courage was a living sermon: Christ is King, and His church will not be chained.

These men stand as a blazing contrast to the majority who folded. Their example is a reminder that when shepherds stand on Scripture, wolves scatter. They proved that faith isn't theory—it's a fight. In the darkest hour, they fought well.

But if bold pastors stood as lights in the storm, the medical establishment became willing tools of darkness. While the pulpits of compromise went quiet, hospitals and health agencies found their voice—not for truth, but for propaganda.

The Lockdowns and Mask Mandates Were Just the Beginning

The lockdowns and mask mandates were never the endgame. They were just the dress rehearsal—the warm-up act before the real show. And behind the curtain pulling the strings? Democrats.

It was Democrats who seized COVID as their golden opportunity to play god. They shut down schools, crushed small businesses, and locked churches while liquor stores and pot shops thrived. Gavin Newsom, Andrew Cuomo, Gretchen Whitmer, Nancy Pelosi—they weren't saving lives, they were tightening their grip. Every decree was about testing the boundaries of compliance. How far will Americans bend before they finally break?

Masks were nothing more than symbols of submission, demanded by Democrats who exempted themselves whenever it suited them. They dined in fancy restaurants while you ate in silence at home. They got their hair styled in private salons while you couldn't even sit at your dying grandmother's bedside. It was never about "safety." It was always about power—Democrat power.

The real battlefield, though, wasn't the masks. It was what came next. The Democrats weren't satisfied with temporary obedience; they wanted permanent allegiance. They needed something to mark the faithful, something to divide the nation, something to brand the compliant and punish the defiant.

That something was the vaccine.

The Mandates

When the vaccines finally rolled out, it wasn't an invitation—it was a demand. And the Democrats were holding the whip. Their message was simple: take the jab, or else.

It was Democrat governors and mayors who signed the orders that crushed Americans. Andrew Cuomo in New York, Gavin Newsom in California, Gretchen Whitmer in Michigan, Lori Lightfoot in Chicago—all of them ruling like little tyrants. These weren't leaders acting in good faith. These were power-drunk politicians who saw COVID as their golden ticket to control.

Workers were forced to comply or lose their jobs. Teachers, nurses, and first responders—purged. Police officers, firefighters, even the military—stripped of careers they had devoted their lives to. The very people Democrats had once praised as "essential" were now disposable because they dared to resist.

And then came the Democrat creation of vaccine passports. Suddenly, the land of the free was divided into two Americas: the "clean" and the "unclean." The obedient, and the rebels. Citizens who had the government's stamp of approval, and those who did not. Democrats had reinvented segregation under the banner of health—something they swore they'd never stand for, yet proudly enforced when it served their agenda.

Families were torn apart. Businesses shuttered. Entire industries bled workers overnight. Hospitals were gutted because nurses wouldn't bow to their authoritarian grip. School districts lost teachers by the thousands. And churches? Many pastors betrayed their flocks, parroting the government's line instead of God's truth.

To make matters worse, Democrats even stooped to bribery. Free beer, free donuts, fast-food gift cards, and even million-dollar lotteries were handed out as bait. It was cheap manipulation dressed up as generosity—a campaign of payoffs designed to manufacture obedience.

Christian leaders were swept into this current. Franklin Graham went so far as to claim that if Jesus were alive today, He would take the vaccine. To hear such words from a respected pastor blurred the lines between faith and propaganda, leaving many believers confused and betrayed. Instead of shepherding the flock toward courage, voices like Graham's reinforced Democrat talking points and lent spiritual cover to Big Pharma's agenda.

This wasn't about science. It was about control—the Democratic machine's control. They used fear like a weapon. They used mandates like chains. They used passports like whips. And America—the so-called land of liberty—became a testing ground for tyranny.

The lockdowns were meant to weaken us. The mandates were meant to break us. And every step of the way, the party's stranglehold was tightening.

Fauci & Big Pharma

Every movement has its high priest, and for Democrats, his name was Anthony Fauci. With television cameras as his pulpit, he preached the gospel of "Science™" while shifting his story more times than the weather. One day masks were useless, the next they were sacred. One day vaccines were the finish line, the next day you'd need "boosters forever." His word was treated as law, not because it was consistent or credible, but because it gave Democrats the excuse they craved: unlimited control.

Fauci was the perfect tool. He spoke with smug certainty, belittling anyone who dared question him, while Democrats held him up as the oracle of truth. To oppose Fauci was to be branded a heretic. He became the poster boy of the pandemic—the "infallible" expert Democrats could hide behind while they crushed dissent.

And while Fauci was playing high priest, Big Pharma was playing banker. Pfizer, Moderna, Johnson & Johnson—companies with rap sheets of corruption longer than some crime syndicates—were suddenly hailed as saviors. Emergency Use Authorizations were rushed through with barely a glance at long-term testing. Safety concerns were swept under the rug. Why? Because billions of dollars were at stake.

The Democrats lined up right behind them. Every mandate, every order, every jab pushed by government just so happened to pad the pockets of their donors. It wasn't about protecting you. It was about protecting the profit pipeline. Fauci got fame, Pharma got fortune, and Democrats got power. The only thing the American people got was betrayal.

They told us the shot was our ticket back to normal life. They said it with straight faces, as if selling snake oil in a new bottle. In reality, it was the oldest political trick in the book: crisis as cover, control as cure. Democrats sold the vaccine not as medicine, but as obedience in a syringe.

And Americans lined up. Some from fear, others from pressure, many from blind trust in a corrupt system. It was the perfect storm—science, money, and politics fused into one machine of manipulation.

But as we would soon learn, this so-called "miracle" came with a terrible price.

The Failure and the Blood

The Democrats promised freedom if we just obeyed. They told us, "Get the shot and life goes back to normal." It was marketed as the ticket to safety, the golden key to unlock society. They dangled our freedoms in front of us like hostages—comply, and you might get them back.

It was a scam.

The so-called "vaccine" failed before it even began. People lined up by the millions, convinced they were being protected, yet breakthrough cases exploded almost immediately. The politicians and their media lapdogs shifted the goalposts overnight—first it was "You won't get COVID," then "You won't spread it," then "You won't get seriously ill." Every promise collapsed under the weight of reality.

Then came the endless boosters. First two shots, then a "top off," then another, then another. It was never enough. What was sold as protection became a revolving door of injections, each one enriching Big Pharma while ordinary Americans were treated like lab rats in a never-ending trial.

Worse still, the Democrats used this failure to divide the nation. Those who complied were hailed as virtuous citizens, parading their vaccine cards like badges of honor. Those who resisted were demonized—called selfish, dangerous, even un-American. Families split, friendships ended, churches fractured. Christians who should have trusted God's providence surrendered instead to fear of losing jobs or social approval, forgetting that obedience to man is disobedience to Christ when man commands what God forbids.

Meanwhile, the unvaccinated carried the weight of ridicule, lost livelihoods, and public shaming. They were labeled the problem—even though the vaccinated were still catching COVID, still transmitting it, and still getting sick in record numbers.

The shot didn't bring back freedom. It didn't end the pandemic. What it did was expose their iron-fisted rule and willingness to lie, to manipulate, and to weaponize fear. They replaced faith with coercion, truth with propaganda, and turned America into a battlefield between the compliant and the courageous.

But the lies were only the beginning. What came next was blood.

Reports of injury and death began to surface almost immediately. Healthy men and women collapsed within days of taking the shot. Young athletes—the very picture of vitality— suddenly dropped dead on basketball courts, football fields, and soccer pitches. Families buried sons and daughters who were supposed to have decades ahead of them. Parents wept over teenagers who had heart inflammation after a "safe" injection. Mothers grieved miscarriages after being told the vaccine was "completely safe" during pregnancy. The grief was unspeakable, yet the government and media dismissed it all as "rare coincidences."

The VAERS database[14], designed to track vaccine injuries, lit up like never before in history. Tens of thousands of reports flooded in: strokes, blood clots, myocarditis, neurological damage, and death. By its own admission, VAERS is vastly underreported[15], meaning the real toll was likely far higher. Yet instead of sounding alarms, health officials buried the data. They treated grieving families as if their pain was inconvenient—as if their loved ones had to die quietly for the sake of the narrative.

Meanwhile, Big Pharma washed its hands of responsibility. Shielded by government contracts, Pfizer, Moderna, and Johnson & Johnson faced zero liability for injuries or deaths. Not a penny in damages could be claimed by the families left shattered. Ordinary citizens carried the weight of funerals, hospital bills, and lifetimes of regret, while corporate executives cashed in record profits.

And where was the mainstream media? They were not watchdogs—they were bodyguards for the Democrat agenda. CNN, MSNBC, The New York Times, and the rest acted like extensions of the Democratic Party[17]. They silenced stories of vaccine injury, mocked grieving parents, and smeared whistleblowers. Night after night, Americans were told "safe and effective" while their neighbors collapsed. The news that should have shaken the nation was buried under propaganda.

Truth only survived through the cracks. Social media became the underground railroad of information, the only place where videos of athletes collapsing, funeral directors speaking out, and doctors warning of danger could be seen. Even then, Facebook, Twitter, and YouTube worked hand-in-hand with the government to censor, shadow-ban, and erase inconvenient truths. Accounts were deleted, posts removed, and voices silenced—but the blood on the ground could not be hidden forever.

This was not medicine. It was betrayal. People trusted their leaders, their doctors, even their pastors, only to be handed a syringe that carried death instead of life. America witnessed a silent massacre, one covered not by news cameras but by hashtags, heartbroken Facebook posts, and obituaries that quietly read "died suddenly."

Democrats, who screamed about "every life matters" during COVID briefings, turned cold when those lives were lost to their so-called cure. They locked arms with the pharmaceutical giants, pretended the deaths were imaginary, and labeled grieving families as conspiracy theorists. It was cruelty layered on top of tragedy.

The cost in blood cannot be measured in statistics alone. It lives in the empty chairs at dinner tables, the father who isn't there to walk his daughter down the aisle, the son who never came home from practice, the newborn who never took its first breath. This was not a "side effect." This was a holocaust of lies, purchased with human souls, and covered with government protection.

It is impossible to look at the carnage and call it anything but what it was: a crime against humanity, carried out under the banner of "science," and baptized in the language of safety.

The country was promised salvation, but what it received was death.

A Nation Divided and Silenced

If the vaccine itself scarred bodies, the mandates scarred the soul of the nation. America, once proud of its freedom, was split in two by the Democrat regime: the "clean" versus the "unclean," the "good citizens" versus the "selfish." It wasn't science that divided us—it was politics.

Families, churches, and workplaces were torn apart. The jab didn't just split medical opinions; it split the nation itself. Spouses fought, siblings stopped speaking, friendships ended. At the dinner table, one side was branded "selfish killers" while the other was condemned as "brainwashed sheep." America's unity was shredded not by a virus, but by Democrat mandates.

Grandparents refused to hug unvaccinated grandchildren. Brothers and sisters stopped speaking. Parents told adult children they were "not welcome" unless they showed proof of vaccination. Weddings, funerals, and birthdays became Gestapo-style checkpoints of compliance. A wedge was driven straight into the heart of American homes.

The bullying was relentless. The vaccinated mocked and belittled the unvaccinated, parroting Democrat talking points that those who refused were "killing grandma," "anti-science," or even "domestic terrorists." Social media became a battlefield of insults and shaming. Neighbors turned on neighbors, friends turned into enemies, churches fractured down the middle.

Perhaps the greatest tragedy was within the Body of Christ. Instead of standing on faith that God would protect, many Christians bowed to fear. They placed their trust not in the Almighty, but in the government. Jobs and positions were valued above obedience to God. Fear of unemployment outweighed faith in divine provision. The words of Christ—"And do not fear those who kill the body but cannot kill the soul. But rather fear Him who is able to destroy both soul and body in hell" (Matthew 10:28)—were forgotten, replaced by fear of a pink slip.

Democrats exploited this division with precision. They weaponized fear and shame, using it to build compliance. They knew exactly what they were doing. By turning American against American, Christian against Christian, they ensured obedience not to God, but to government.

And perhaps the cruelest irony of all? The very people who screamed "My body, my choice" when it came to abortion suddenly abandoned that principle when it came to vaccines. The same Democrats who demanded autonomy for the killing of unborn children now denied autonomy to the living, forcing injections into the arms of those who said no. The hypocrisy was staggering, but the media never blinked.

The saddest part is how many mindless sheep went along with it. They traded freedom for false safety, parroted propaganda without question, and mocked those who stood firm. Instead of discernment, they chose blind obedience. Instead of courage, they chose compliance. Instead of faith, they chose fear.

This was not the America our forefathers bled for. It was an America reprogrammed by fear, divided by lies, and reshaped into something unrecognizable. The damage lingers still—in broken families, fractured churches, and friendships that may never recover.

But the division wasn't enough for them. Those who refused to break had to be silenced.

If the mandates divided America, the silencing of dissent finished the job. The Democrats, aided by their loyal extension—the mainstream media—launched an all-out assault on anyone who dared question their narrative.

Doctors who spent their lives in medicine suddenly became enemies of the state. Men like Dr. Robert Malone, the very inventor of mRNA technology, was cast as a conspiracy theorist when he warned about the dangers. Dr. Peter McCullough, one of the most published cardiologists in the world, was stripped of credibility and censored for daring to point out the risks. Dr. Simone Gold, who stood boldly against the lies, was arrested and publicly smeared. These were not fringe voices. They were experts—silenced because they refused to bow.

And it wasn't just doctors. Everyday citizens—teachers, soldiers, pastors, mothers, fathers—anyone who raised a red flag was shadow-banned, deplatformed, or publicly shamed. Posts disappeared overnight. Videos were pulled down. Accounts were locked. Truth became contraband.

I know this firsthand. People like me, who spoke out against mandates, found themselves blacklisted. I was shadow-banned. Others were expelled from platforms altogether. Ordinary Americans were treated like criminals simply for asking questions.

Mainstream media did not expose this—they buried it. CNN, MSNBC, The New York Times, all mouthpieces of the Democratic Party, acted as gatekeepers of propaganda. They called dissenters "dangerous," "anti-science," "misinformation spreaders." Meanwhile, the truth only survived through whispers on social media—Twitter threads, Telegram channels, podcasts—fragile pipelines constantly under threat of being cut off. For many, these shadowy corners of the internet were the only way to see what was really happening.

Think about that: in America, the land of free speech, the truth was banned. A Democrat-run censorship regime decided who could speak, who could publish, who could even exist online. Doctors silenced. Pastors silenced. Citizens silenced. The First Amendment shredded in the name of "safety."

This wasn't health policy. It was tyranny in a lab coat. It was obedience enforced through fear and silence. And the church, instead of rising in outrage, too often shrugged and moved on.

History will record that truth itself was put on trial during COVID—and under Democrat rule, it was found guilty and executed.

The mandates didn't just scar bodies. They scarred the nation's soul.

The Spiritual Reality

What happened during COVID was never just political. It was never just medical. It was spiritual to the core.

Democrats dressed it up in lab coats and executive orders, but underneath it all was a war against God. The vaccine rollout, the mandates, the silencing of truth-tellers—every piece of it was engineered to replace faith in Christ with faith in the state. It was a satanic counterfeit, a cheap imitation of trust in God, rebranded as "trust the science."

And tragically, millions of Christians bowed. They feared man more than they feared God. They believed Fauci more than they believed Scripture. They clung to their jobs, their reputations, and their security, rather than clinging to the One who promised never to leave nor forsake them. The church that was supposed to roar like a lion became a flock of mindless sheep, bleating on command at the voice of politicians.

This was the devil's playbook in plain sight. Where Christ calls His people to courage, Democrats called them to compliance. Where God says "Fear not," Democrats trafficked in fear as their currency. Where Jesus promised freedom, Democrats offered chains—chains of mandates, chains of passports, chains of social approval.

This was not just a public health policy. It was a spiritual test. Would God's people trust Him? Or would they trust the system? The answer, for most, is heartbreaking. They chose Caesar. They chose safety. They chose slavery.

But a remnant remained. A faithful few refused to bow, not because they were reckless, but because they knew where true salvation lies. They stood as living testimonies that Christ is King and no mandate can overrule His Word.

COVID was never just about a virus. It was about worship. And America failed the test.

The Blueprint of Tyranny

Satan's blueprint was laid bare for the whole world to see, and the Democrats—along with liberal politicians across the globe—seized the opportunity. COVID was not just a virus; it was a stage, a test run, a carefully designed pattern of control. What was revealed in those years was nothing less than a sketch of the coming One World Order, a glimpse of how fear, obedience, and deception could enslave entire nations without a single bullet being fired.

And the frightening part? It worked. Entire populations surrendered their freedoms with barely a protest. People traded liberty for a false sense of security, freedom of worship for the approval of government, and truth for the comfort of propaganda. The pandemic revealed just how easily the masses could be herded, how quickly the so-called "land of the free" could be transformed into a land of mandates, checkpoints, and compliance.

If this was only a blueprint, what will happen when the real structure is built? When the next global crisis comes—whether health, economic, or environmental—will the people of God stand firm, or will they bow once again to fear? If we could not stand against vaccine mandates, how will we stand against the

Beast system when refusal to comply means not just losing a job, but losing the right to buy, sell, or even exist within society?

The church must face this sobering reality: if we crumbled under COVID, how will we endure when true persecution comes? If pulpits went silent in the face of lockdowns, what will happen when the gospel itself is outlawed? If Christians could not withstand the pressure of Democrat politicians wielding masks and passports, what will happen when the pressure is global, total, and eternal?

Perhaps the lesson is this: COVID was not merely a tragedy, it was a warning. A wake-up call. A glimpse of the spiritual war unfolding before our eyes. Satan does not hide his schemes—he practices them openly, counting on the church to slumber while he lays the groundwork. Democrats and their allies may believe they are engineers of progress, but in truth, they are unwitting builders of a kingdom that opposes Christ.

The question remains: will the church learn from this? Will believers recognize that the next storm will be even greater, and that faith must be anchored not in the state, not in politicians, not in science, but in Christ alone? Because if we did not stand then, we will not stand tomorrow. And if we do not awaken now, the One World Order will not be a future threat—it will be our present reality.

COVID revealed how quickly Americans would trade freedom for false safety. But the groundwork for that surrender was laid years earlier through another deception—the gospel of "social justice." While Christians slept, Democrats replaced biblical justice with a counterfeit that divides by race, rewards lawlessness, and calls evil good. They turned justice into a weapon against the very people it should protect.

PM Kimbler

Chapter 7: Social Justice and Biblical Justice

They burned cities in the name of "justice." Minneapolis, Portland, Kenosha—billions in damage, dozens dead, thousands of livelihoods destroyed. Democrats called it "mostly peaceful protests." They bailed out the rioters. They painted "Black Lives Matter" on the streets while black-owned businesses smoldered in the background.

This isn't justice. It's vengeance wearing a mask.

God's justice builds up. Democrat "justice" burns down.

The Democratic Party has taken the language of "justice" and twisted it into something that looks nothing like God's truth. They call it "social justice," but it divides instead of unites. It rewards groups instead of judging fairly. It stirs up bitterness instead of calling for repentance. It's a man-made system propped up by grievance and guilt, and it cannot stand before God's throne.

God's Justice vs. Man's Justice

God tells us exactly what justice looks like. "He has shown you, O man, what is good; and what does the Lord require of you but to do justly, to love mercy, and to walk humbly with your God?" (Micah 6:8). Justice in God's eyes is rooted in truth and humility, not favoritism or politics.

That's why Proverbs 21:15 tells us, "It is a joy for the just to do justice, but destruction will come to the workers of iniquity." True justice brings peace because it upholds righteousness. It doesn't bend for political gain. It doesn't shift with culture. It doesn't play favorites.

But the Democrats push a justice that flips God's standard upside down. They excuse sin, reward lawlessness, and even call evil good. They have crafted a false justice that makes the guilty comfortable and the righteous uneasy. That is not justice—it's rebellion against God's throne.

A Shameful History, An Unrepentant Spirit

We can't ignore history. The Democratic Party was the party of slavery, of segregation, of the KKK. That's not rumor—that's fact. Instead of repentance, they rewrote their story and tried to put themselves in the hero's role.

"I acknowledged my sin to You, and my iniquity I have not hidden. I said, 'I will confess my transgressions to the Lord,' and You forgave the iniquity of my sin" (Psalm 32:5). That's what real repentance looks like—bringing darkness into the light and finding forgiveness.

But the Democrats never confessed. They simply rebranded. They went from open chains to hidden chains—chains of dependency, bitterness, and generational resentment. They never said, "We were wrong." They just found new ways to control people under the banner of compassion.

And here's the danger: when sin goes unconfessed, it resurfaces. Their modern obsession with identity politics and racial division is just yesterday's prejudice repackaged. It's the same old sin with a new label.

Equity vs. Righteousness

One of their favorite words today is "equity." It sounds noble, but don't be fooled. Equity isn't the same as equality. Equality is a biblical principle—equal treatment, equal opportunity under the law. Equity is a man-made distortion that demands equal outcomes, no matter the cost.

God warns us against this in Leviticus 19:15: "You shall do no injustice in judgment. You shall not be partial to the poor or defer to the great, but in righteousness you shall judge your neighbor." Notice that God doesn't say "tilt the scales to even things out." He says, "Judge righteously."

But Democrats tilt the scales constantly. DEI programs, hiring quotas, race-based admissions—they call it compassion, but in reality, it destroys standards, robs people of true achievement, and creates resentment. Biblical justice judges each person by truth and character; Democrat justice judges by skin color and group identity.

Repentance vs. Grievance

Here's the biggest difference between biblical justice and social justice: biblical justice looks to the heart, while social justice looks to history.

God says in Isaiah 55:7, "Let the wicked forsake his way, and the unrighteous man his thoughts; let him return to the Lord, that He may have mercy on him, and to our God, for He will abundantly pardon." Repentance brings forgiveness. It heals wounds. It restores relationships.

But Democrats cling to grievance. They keep past sins alive by constantly reopening old wounds—slavery, segregation, systemic guilt. They turn history into a weapon. Instead of pointing people to repentance and restoration in Christ, they pit groups against one another and hand out blame like it's justice.

That isn't healing. It's poison. And the fruit is clear: division, resentment, suspicion, and endless anger.

False Compassion

Democrats love to cloak their policies in compassion. They say, "We're doing this to help the marginalized." But real compassion never contradicts truth.

"Open rebuke is better than love carefully concealed" (Proverbs 27:5). Real love tells the truth. Real compassion doesn't excuse sin; it calls people out of it.

But Democrats use compassion as a smokescreen. They excuse irresponsibility. They lower standards. They treat people as permanent victims who can never rise. That's not compassion—that's control. It's keeping people dependent instead of setting them free.

Biblical compassion lifts people up, equips them, and points them to responsibility and dignity in Christ. Anything less is counterfeit.

What's Really at Stake

This isn't just about policies or platforms—it's about souls. Because once a society redefines justice, it redefines righteousness. And when righteousness is redefined, truth collapses.

"The righteous and the wicked are an abomination to each other" (Proverbs 29:27). Justice is a dividing line. You can't stand in both camps. You can't embrace a party that warps God's standard of justice and claim to be standing with Christ.

The Democrats' version of justice is seductive because it sounds compassionate. But it is nothing less than rebellion against God's holy standard.

The Church's Call

We are not called to be silent spectators. "And have no fellowship with the unfruitful works of darkness, but rather expose them" (Ephesians 5:11). That's the Church's role in this moment—to expose false justice for what it is and to call people back to God's eternal standard.

That means pastors can't stay quiet. Christians can't shrug their shoulders. Every believer is called to shine light in a culture that confuses justice with partiality and compassion with compromise.

Your Moment of Decision

At the end of the day, the question is simple: Will you stand with God's definition of justice, or with man's counterfeit version?

"For the Lord loves justice; He will not forsake His saints. They are preserved forever, but the descendants of the wicked shall be cut off" (Psalm 37:28). God will always stand with those who stand with His truth.

The Democrats' social justice divides, destroys, and deceives. God's justice restores, redeems, and unites. You can't follow both. You must choose.

When you step into the voting booth, you're not just making a political choice—you're making a moral one. Will you stand for righteousness, or will you lend your voice to a counterfeit?

The river of God's justice is flowing. Step into it. Let it wash away the lies of man-made justice. And let your life, and your vote, declare that God's standard is the only one that stands forever.

But false justice needs enforcement, and that's where government comes in. The same Democrats who pervert justice have perverted government itself—transforming it from God's servant into a would-be god. They've forgotten the most basic truth: all authority comes from above, and those who wield it will answer for how they used it.

Chapter 8: The Role of Government and Biblical Authority

Biden just said it out loud: "We the people" means the government.

That's not a slip of the tongue. That's the Democratic creed. They've replaced the Constitution's vision of citizen sovereignty with a new religion: the all-powerful state. Your rights don't come from God anymore—they come from Washington. Your freedom isn't inherent—it's granted by politicians. Your children belong to "the village," not to you.

This is the Democratic vision: Government as God.

But that's not what Scripture teaches.

The Bible lays out a clear framework for government: it exists to protect the innocent, punish evil, and uphold justice under God's authority. Nothing more, nothing less.

But the Democratic Party has embraced a vision of government that rivals God Himself. They see government as the solution to every problem, the answer to every question, and the authority over every decision. Instead of protecting freedom, they seek to redefine it. Instead of defending faith, they silence it. Instead of guarding families, they undermine them.

God's Blueprint for Government

The Bible makes it clear that government is not a human invention—it's God's. Yet He gave it very narrow boundaries.

"Let every soul be subject to the governing authorities. For there is no authority except from God, and the authorities that exist are appointed by God" (Romans 13:1).

Notice: authority comes from God, not from the will of the people, not from party platforms, not from Washington. Government is God's servant, not His competitor.

"Learn to do good; seek justice, correct oppression; defend the fatherless, plead for the widow" (Isaiah 1:17). That is the spirit that should guide every ruler.

But humility is not what we see in modern politics—especially in the Democratic Party. What we see is pride, overreach, and the constant attempt to replace God's authority with government mandates.

Boundaries God Established

God didn't just say what government should do—He also made clear what it should not do. When Israel demanded a king in 1 Samuel 8, God warned that a ruler who expanded beyond His boundaries would burden the people, take their children, tax their goods, and enslave their freedoms. That's exactly what happens when government grows beyond its God-given role.

"It is better to trust in the Lord than to put confidence in princes" (Psalm 118:9). Every time a nation looks to politicians to solve spiritual problems, disaster follows.

This is why the Democratic platform is so dangerous. Their policies extend government control into family life, religious practice, education, healthcare, and even personal conscience. They erase God's limits and put man in His place.

America's Foundation: Freedom Under God

The founding of our nation wasn't perfect, but its backbone was built on a biblical principle: freedom comes from God, not from government. The Declaration of Independence says it plainly— "endowed by their Creator with certain unalienable Rights."

Early Americans understood what we often forget today: if rights come from government, government can take them away. But if rights come from God, no politician can strip them from you.

That's why the First Amendment starts with protecting religion and speech. The Founders knew that without the freedom to worship God and to speak truth, no other freedoms could last.

"Righteousness exalts a nation, but sin is a reproach to any people" (Proverbs 14:34). When a government honors God's authority, a nation thrives. When it rejects Him, it crumbles.

The Democratic Overreach

The Democratic Party has traded America's founding vision for something very different. They expand government into every corner of life while shrinking the role of faith and family.

They redefine freedom as the "right" to abortion and gender ideology while restricting the right to pray, preach, or parent according to God's Word.

They promote economic dependency on government programs instead of personal responsibility and stewardship.

They impose regulations that strangle small businesses and families while claiming it's for the "greater good."

"Woe to those who call evil good, and good evil; who put darkness for light, and light for darkness; who put bitter for sweet, and sweet for bitter!" (Isaiah 5:20). That's the moral collapse we are watching play out under Democratic policies.

The Church's Response

Throughout history, God's people have resisted governments that tried to exalt themselves above Him. Daniel refused to bow to Nebuchadnezzar. Peter and John told the Sanhedrin, "We ought to obey God rather than men" (Acts 5:29). Early American pastors—known as the "Black Robed Regiment"—preached liberty from their pulpits, fueling the courage of the Revolution.

The church today faces the same calling. We are not called to worship the state, but to speak truth to it. When policies attack worship, undermine parents, and replace God's authority with government control, silence is not an option.

Where You Stand

Here's the bottom line: Government is God's servant, not your savior. Every vote is a declaration of whether you believe that.

"And He changes the times and the seasons; He removes kings and raises up kings; He gives wisdom to the wise and knowledge to those who have understanding" (Daniel 2:21). God is sovereign over all rulers, yet He holds us accountable for who we support. Christians cannot cast their vote for a party that consistently undermines God's order and elevates human authority above divine authority.

The Democratic Party has made its position clear: government over God, state over Scripture, politics over principle. For a follower of Christ, that is not an option.

As believers, we must support leaders who understand that government has boundaries, and those boundaries are set by God Himself. Our hope is not in politicians, but in the King of kings. Yet our responsibility is to vote for those who recognize their accountability before Him.

But when government abandons its God-given boundaries, chaos follows. Nowhere is this more evident than at our borders, where Democratic policies have turned order into anarchy and compassion into cruelty. The blood of innocent Americans cries out from the ground.

PM Kimbler

Chapter 9: Borders, Immigration, and Biblical Law

Twenty-two-year-old Laken Riley went for a jog on her college campus in Georgia. She never came home. Her killer was an illegal immigrant who should have been deported but was shielded by Democratic policies[10].

Twelve-year-old Jocelyn Nungaray was strangled and dumped in a creek in Houston. Her killers? Illegal immigrants released into the country under the Biden-Harris administration[11].

Twenty-year-old Kayla Hamilton was raped and murdered in Maryland by an illegal immigrant who had been arrested before but never deported[12].

These aren't just statistics. They're daughters, sisters, friends—young women whose lives were cut short by policies that put political ideology above public safety. And they are only a few names among countless others whose stories never made the evening news.

Meanwhile, hundreds of thousands of migrant children have simply vanished into the system under Democratic immigration policies[13]. Missing. Gone. Children placed with unvetted adults, handed to traffickers, lost to predators. The Democratic Party calls this "compassion." But tell that to the grieving parents and shattered families. Tell them how compassionate it feels to bury your child.

Does God really want open borders? Does Scripture support policies that ignore laws and endanger the innocent? Does biblical love mean refusing to protect your own citizens? The answer is written clearly in God's Word: He designed nations with borders for a reason. When those boundaries are abandoned, the result is chaos, suffering, and death.

God's Plan for Nations

God didn't create a world without borders—He established them Himself.

"And He has made from one blood every nation of men to dwell on all the face of the earth, and has determined their preappointed times and the boundaries of their dwellings" (Acts 17:26).

God set the boundaries. He drew the lines. Not politicians, not activists, not globalists with good intentions. Borders were His design, meant to maintain order and protect people.

"When the Most High divided their inheritance to the nations, when He separated the sons of Adam, He set the boundaries of the peoples according to the number of the children of Israel" (Deuteronomy 32:8).

But Democrats act as though God's design is flawed. Their platform promotes policies that decriminalize illegal crossings, expand sanctuary cities, and weaken enforcement. And the result has been devastating: communities overwhelmed, cartels emboldened, and innocent blood shed.

"The Lord is King forever and ever; the nations have perished out of His land" (Psalm 10:16). When nations defy His order, they set themselves on a path to destruction.

Compassion Without Law Is Chaos

Christians are often told: "If you love immigrants, you must support open borders." But Scripture never pits compassion against justice.

"The stranger who dwells among you shall be to you as one born among you, and you shall love him as yourself; for you were strangers in the land of Egypt: I am the Lord your God" (Leviticus 19:34). That's true. But "One law shall be for the native-born and for the stranger who dwells among you" (Exodus 12:49) is equally clear.

One law for everyone. That is fairness. That is justice. To ignore this principle is to create lawlessness.

"You shall not show partiality in judgment; you shall hear the small as well as the great; you shall not be afraid in any man's presence, for the judgment is God's" (Deuteronomy 1:17). Yet Democratic policies show partiality by shielding those who break immigration law while punishing citizens with the consequences.

That is not compassion. That is corruption.

The Biden-Harris Border Disaster

Since 2021, there have been more than 7.6 million border encounters[4]—a number greater than the population of Arizona[16]. Another 1.5 million gotaways slipped in undetected. No one knows who they are, where they went, or what they are doing in our neighborhoods.

Even more horrifying is the mass disappearance of migrant children. Tens of thousands unaccounted for, many placed into the hands of cartels and traffickers because the Biden-Harris administration abandoned basic vetting.

This isn't compassion. It's cruelty dressed up in political language. It's policies that sacrifice children to predators and deliver communities to chaos.

Sanctuary Cities: Protecting Criminals, Not Families

Perhaps nowhere is the rebellion against God's design clearer than in so-called "sanctuary cities."

In New York City, Mayor Eric Adams boasts about protecting undocumented immigrants, even as violent crime surges and shelters overflow. In Chicago, Mayor Brandon Johnson pledges to shield illegals while his city bleeds from daily shootings. Boston's Mayor Michelle Wu insists on non-cooperation with ICE, ensuring dangerous criminals walk free. And in California, Governor Gavin Newsom presides over an entire sanctuary state, where police are ordered not to hand offenders over to federal agents—even murderers.

These leaders stand before cameras and call it compassion. But tell that to the families of victims. Tell that to parents who buried their daughters because politicians wanted to score points with activists.

"So you shall not pollute the land where you are; for blood defiles the land, and no atonement can be made for the land, for the blood that is shed on it, except by the blood of him who shed it" (Numbers 35:33).

Sanctuary policies pollute the land with innocent blood. They spit on justice and mock the God who demands it.

The Contrast: Trump vs. Biden

When Donald Trump came into office, he made border security a priority. Crossings plummeted to record lows. Traffickers feared consequences. Law enforcement was empowered to do its job. Communities felt safer because there was a leader willing to enforce God's principle of order.

Now contrast that with the Biden-Harris administration. Crossings at record highs. Children missing. Cartels emboldened. Cities collapsing under the weight of sanctuary lawlessness. Where Trump brought order, Biden has brought chaos. Where Trump put criminals on notice, Biden put out a welcome mat.

The fruit speaks for itself. One leader stood for sovereignty, justice, and safety. The other opened the floodgates to lawlessness.

God's Standard for Nations

"The strength of the King loves justice. You have established equity; You have executed justice and righteousness in Jacob" (Psalm 99:4). God loves justice—and He expects nations to reflect that love by protecting the innocent and punishing the guilty.

To support policies that do the opposite is not merely bad politics—it's rebellion against God Himself.

The Church's Responsibility

Christians cannot sit this one out. We are called to defend the fatherless, to protect the oppressed, and to stand against lawlessness. Remaining silent while politicians abandon justice makes the church complicit in the blood that is shed.

"Where there is no revelation, the people cast off restraint; but happy is he who keeps the law" (Proverbs 29:18).

If we don't speak, if we don't vote in line with God's truth, the lawlessness will only grow worse.

A Call to Action

Every vote is a choice. Either we honor God's design for nations and borders, or we enable rebellion against it.

The Democratic Party has made their choice. They've chosen lawlessness. They've chosen policies that get Americans killed, deliver children to traffickers, and empower criminals.

The choice before Christians is clear: Will we side with God's Word, or with a party platform that mocks His design?

"Listen, O you who know righteousness, you people in whose heart is My law: Do not fear the reproach of men, nor be afraid of their insults" (Isaiah 51:7).

Do not fear being called "heartless" for supporting secure borders. Do not fear being slandered as "unloving" for demanding justice. Fear only this: standing before God one day and having to explain why you supported policies that destroyed lives and shed innocent blood.

Honor God. Protect the innocent. Secure the border. And never forget—the blood of the innocent cries out for justice.

You've seen the evidence. You know what the Democratic Party stands for. Now comes the hardest question of all: If you claim to follow Jesus but keep voting Democrat, is your faith even real?

PM Kimbler

Chapter 10: The Test of True Faith

"I'm a Christian, but I vote Democrat."

Maybe you've said it. Maybe someone close to you has. Maybe you're holding onto it right now, torn between what you believe and what you support.

Friend, this is where honesty matters most. Because here's the truth: you cannot follow Jesus and keep voting for a party that openly rejects Him.

This isn't about being mean. It isn't about condemning people. It's about facing reality. And reality is—the Democratic Party has built its entire platform in direct opposition to the Word of God.

You can't love Jesus and defend abortion. You can't honor Scripture and celebrate same-sex marriage. You can't trust God's design and support open borders that trample His blueprint for nations. You can't claim Christ while standing with leaders who mock His authority.

When Jesus is Lord, He's Lord of everything—including your vote.

The Honesty Test

The Bible doesn't leave room for excuses.

"Now by this we know that we know Him, if we keep His commandments. He who says, 'I know Him,' and does not keep His commandments, is a liar, and the truth is not in him" (1 John 2:3-4).

That's not my opinion. That's Scripture. If someone claims to know Jesus but consistently votes for policies that spit in His face, something is wrong.

James said it too: "But be doers of the word, and not hearers only, deceiving yourselves" (James 1:22).

In other words—don't just talk about Jesus. Live like you believe Him. Even in the voting booth.

Twisting Scripture

Here's how Christian Democrats try to justify the compromise: they twist verses.

Their favorite? "Love your neighbor as yourself."

So they say abortion is "loving women." Same-sex marriage is "love is love." Open borders are "welcoming the stranger."

But they leave out the first commandment: "You shall love the Lord your God with all your heart, with all your soul, and with all your mind."

You can't love your neighbor while ignoring the God who defines love. Real love operates inside His boundaries—not outside of them.

Scripture says we must "rightly dividing the word of truth" (2 Timothy 2:15). But twisting verses to bless sin is not rightly handling anything—it's rebellion dressed in church clothes.

The "Compassion" Lie

Democrats love to cloak sin in the word "compassion."

They'll point to verses about sharing with the poor and claim it justifies massive government programs or open borders. But here's the difference: God calls for personal generosity, not forced redistribution. He calls you and me to share—not for politicians to weaponize taxes and lawlessness.

Compassion without truth isn't compassion. It's betrayal.

Idols in the Party

For some, it's climate. They treat the earth like a god, sacrificing families, jobs, and communities on the altar of "green policy."

For others, it's tolerance. They call it "inclusion," but really it's a refusal to stand for truth. Real love calls sinners to repentance. Fake love pats them on the back all the way to hell.

At the end of the day, it all comes back to the same thing: the Democratic Party has made idols out of sin. And too many Christians are bowing down.

No Such Thing as "Private Faith"

Maybe you've heard this: "My faith is private. It doesn't affect my politics."

But that's nonsense. Jesus asked: "But why do you call Me 'Lord, Lord,' and not do the things which I say?" (Luke 6:46).

If He's really Lord, then nothing is off-limits. Not your wallet. Not your relationships. Not your politics.

Private faith is dead faith. Real faith shows up everywhere—including your vote.

The Eternal Stakes

This isn't just about parties. This is about souls.

When Christians back policies that oppose God, they confuse the watching world. They make unbelievers think Christianity is just another political label. And that destroys the church's witness.

"I know your works, that you are neither cold nor hot. I could wish you were cold or hot. So then, because you are lukewarm, and neither cold nor hot, I will vomit you out of My mouth" (Revelation 3:15-16).

Doing His will means following Him in every area of life—including politics.

The Choice Before You

Here's the hard truth: you can follow Jesus, or you can follow the Democratic Party. But you cannot do both.

You can't serve two masters. You can't split your heart. You can't give Sunday to God and Tuesday to man.

"Happy are those who keep His testimonies, who seek Him with the whole heart!" (Psalm 119:2).

Whole heart—not half. Whole heart—not compartmentalized. Whole heart—not "Jesus on Sunday, Democrats on Tuesday."

What Real Faith Looks Like

- Real faith protects innocent life.
- Real faith honors marriage as God designed it.
- Real faith seeks justice based on truth, not identity politics.
- Real faith calls people to work and responsibility, not dependency.
- Real faith loves the poor by giving generously—not by letting politicians weaponize "compassion" for power.

That's what obedience looks like. That's what faith that doesn't compromise looks like.

Your Moment of Truth

Isaiah said it plainly: "The grass withers, the flower fades, but the word of our God stands forever" (Isaiah 40:8).

Parties rise and fall. Platforms change. But God's Word never moves.

So here's the question: will your loyalty be to a party, or to the King of Kings?

The Democratic Party has made its choice. They've rejected Him. Now the choice is yours.

Will you keep excusing, twisting, and compartmentalizing?

Or will you surrender—your whole heart, your whole life, your whole vote—to Jesus Christ?

The answer to that question reveals the authenticity of your faith.

Choose wisely. Eternity is watching.

This book has laid out the evidence. The Democratic Party stands against everything God stands for. Now it's time for action. It's time to live what you claim to believe. It's time for faithful citizenship with no compromise.

Chapter 11: A Call to Faithful Citizenship

You've reached the final chapter. But this isn't the end of the book—it's the beginning of a decision that will mark your soul and your legacy.

Now you know the truth. The mask is off. The Democratic Party is not just a different political opinion—it is an outright rebellion against the God of Scripture. They defend abortion, celebrate sin, mock marriage, undermine work, silence faith, and trample freedom. They exalt the state in the place of God.

So the question isn't: Do you know enough?

The question is: What will you do with what you know?

The Weight of Your Choice

Scripture makes it plain: "I have chosen the way of truth; Your judgments I have laid before me" (Psalm 119:30).

Notice the word chosen. Faith isn't a label you wear—it's a choice you live. And that choice shows up in the voting booth just as much as it does in church on Sunday.

You cannot serve two masters. You cannot love the Lord with your lips and then vote for leaders who mock His Word. You cannot claim to walk in the light while casting your lot with darkness.

This is not politics. This is discipleship.

Beyond the Ballot

Faithful citizenship is more than one day in November. It's a way of life.

Pray for your leaders. Even the ones you didn't vote for. Even the ones who oppose God. Pray for their repentance. Pray for their hearts to turn. "Therefore I exhort first of all that supplications, prayers, intercessions, and giving of thanks be made for all men, for kings and all who are in authority, that we may lead a quiet and peaceable life in all godliness and reverence" (1 Timothy 2:1-2).

Speak the truth. Don't be silent when God's Word is trampled in public life. Don't shrink back when truth is mocked in schools, workplaces, or even churches. "I will speak of Your testimonies also before kings, and will not be ashamed" (Psalm 119:46).

Teach your children. Don't let them grow up in confusion. Don't leave their worldview to TikTok, Netflix, or government schools. Teach them diligently the truth of God's Word and how to live it out. "And these words which I command you today shall be in your heart. You shall teach them diligently to your children, and shall talk of them when you sit in your house, when you walk by the way, when you lie down, and when you rise up" (Deuteronomy 6:6-7).

Stand firm when the tide rises. The world will call you extreme. Weak churches will call you divisive. Family may call you judgmental. But God calls you faithful. "I can do all things through Christ who strengthens me" (Philippians 4:13).

Hope for America

We are not writing the obituary of America—we are writing the invitation to revival.

God still heals nations. "If My people who are called by My name will humble themselves, and pray and seek My face, and turn from their wicked ways, then I will hear from heaven, and will forgive their sin and heal their land" (2 Chronicles 7:14).

But notice—it doesn't start with Congress. It doesn't start with the White House. It starts with God's people. It starts with you.

No Compromise

This book has carried one message from beginning to end: No Compromise.

- No compromise with abortion.
- No compromise with redefining marriage.
- No compromise with silencing faith.
- No compromise with putting government where only God belongs.

Jesus said: "If you love Me, keep My commandments" (John 14:15).

That's not optional. That's not negotiable. That's not subject to political convenience.

No compromise means following Jesus with your whole heart—including your vote.

Your Defining Moment

This is it. This is the line in the sand.

You can walk away from this book and keep your politics the same, but you cannot say you didn't know. You cannot say no one told you. You cannot say your conscience wasn't warned.

"Not everyone who says to Me, 'Lord, Lord,' shall enter the kingdom of heaven, but he who does the will of My Father in heaven" (Matthew 7:21).

Doing His will includes every ballot you cast, every policy you support, every leader you endorse.

Eternity is watching. Your children are watching. And above all—God is watching.

The Final Word

The Democrats have made their choice. They have chosen rebellion against God.

Now it's time for you to make yours.

Will you stand with Jesus, or will you stand with those who mock Him?

Will you choose the eternal Word of God, or the temporary politics of man?

Will you live by No Compromise, or die by compromise?

The time for excuses is over. The time for silence is over. The time for compromise is over.

Stand firm. Speak truth. Vote faithfully. Live boldly.

NO COMPROMISE.

PM Kimbler

DISCUSSION QUESTIONS

Chapter 1: The Authority of Scripture

1. How do you personally handle it when Scripture conflicts with popular culture? Give a specific example.

2. The chapter mentions Christians who "pick and choose" which parts of God's Word to obey. In what areas might you be guilty of this?

3. What does it mean practically that "voting is worship"? How should this change how you approach elections?

4. Discuss the statement: "You can't champion one Bible truth while ignoring others." How does this apply to political issues?

5. What are some ways Christians justify compromise, and why are these justifications dangerous?

Chapter 2: Abortion and the Sanctity of Life

1. How would you respond to someone who says, "I'm personally pro-life, but I don't want to impose my beliefs on others"?

2. Discuss the stories shared in this chapter (Juda Myers, Cristiano Ronaldo, the author's granddaughter). How do they counter common pro-abortion arguments?

3. The chapter calls abortion "ancient evil in modern practice." What parallels do you see between today's abortion industry and biblical child sacrifice?

4. How should Christians respond to the "rape and incest" argument while maintaining compassion for victims?

5. What practical steps can your church take to support life beyond just voting?

Chapter 3: Marriage, Sexuality, and Gender

1. Why is the redefinition of marriage not just a "live and let live" issue for Christians?

2. How do you biblically respond to the argument that "love is love"?

3. Discuss the "slippery slope" argument. Do you see evidence of this progression in current culture?

4. How should Christians interact with transgender individuals while maintaining biblical truth?

5. What does it mean that marriage "reflects the mystery of Christ and His church"?

Chapter 4: Economic Policies and Biblical Stewardship

1. How do you distinguish between biblical charity and government welfare programs?

2. Discuss this statement: "Democrats have replaced God with government." Do you agree? Why or why not?

3. How should Christians view work, and how does this impact political choices?

4. What does the Bible teach about debt, both personal and national?

5. How can Christians help the poor in ways that honor God's design?

Chapter 5: Religious Liberty and Free Speech

1. Should Christians keep their faith "private" to avoid offending others? Why or why not?
2. How do you respond when accused of "imposing your beliefs" on others through political action?
3. Discuss examples of Christians being persecuted for their beliefs in America today.
4. What does it mean to "fear God, not the focus group"?
5. How can the church prepare for increased persecution?

Chapter 6: COVID-19

1. How did your church respond during COVID lockdowns? Looking back, what would you change?
2. Discuss the balance between obeying government (Romans 13) and obeying God (Acts 5:29).
3. What lessons should Christians learn from the COVID response for future crises?
4. How did fear vs. faith play out during the pandemic in your community?
5. What warning signs should Christians watch for regarding government overreach?

Chapter 7: Social Justice and Biblical Justice

1. How do you distinguish between biblical justice and "social justice"?

2. Discuss the statement: "God's justice builds up. Democrat 'justice' burns down."

3. How should Christians approach issues of racial reconciliation biblically?

4. What's the difference between equality and equity? Which is biblical?

5. How can the church promote true justice in our communities?

Chapter 8: The Role of Government and Biblical Authority

1. What are the biblical boundaries of government authority?

2. How do you respond to Christians who say, "Jesus wasn't political"?

3. Discuss the founders' vision of rights coming from God vs. government. Why does this matter?

4. When is civil disobedience biblically justified?

5. How can Christians influence government while avoiding the temptation to make politics an idol?

Chapter 9: Borders, Immigration, and Biblical Law

1. How do you balance biblical compassion for immigrants with support for border security?

2. Discuss the difference between legal and illegal immigration from a biblical perspective.

3. How do "sanctuary city" policies violate biblical principles of justice?

4. What does the Bible teach about national sovereignty and borders?

5. How can Christians minister to immigrants while supporting lawful immigration?

Chapter 10: The Test of True Faith

1. The chapter asks: "If you claim to follow Jesus but keep voting Democrat, is your faith even real?" How do you respond to this challenge?

2. Discuss ways Christians twist Scripture to justify unbiblical political positions.

3. What does it mean that "private faith is dead faith"?

4. How do you handle relationships with family and friends who disagree with your political positions?

5. What evidence in your life demonstrates that Jesus is truly Lord over everything?

Chapter 11: A Call to Faithful Citizenship

1. What does "faithful citizenship" look like beyond just voting?

2. How do you maintain hope for America while acknowledging our moral decline?

3. Discuss practical ways to influence politics at local, state, and federal levels.

4. What would revival look like in America today?

5. How will you apply what you've learned from this book in the next election cycle?

APPENDICES

Appendix A: What They Say vs. What the Bible Says

Democratic Talking Point: "Love Your Neighbor"

What They Say: "Jesus said to love your neighbor, so we should support open borders, same-sex marriage, and unlimited government assistance."

What the Bible Actually Says: "If you love Me, keep My commandments" (John 14:15). Love operates within God's boundaries, not against them. Real love tells the truth and upholds God's design.

Democratic Talking Point: "Don't Judge"

What They Say: "Jesus said don't judge, so Christians shouldn't oppose abortion, homosexuality, or transgender ideology."

What the Bible Actually Says: "Do not judge according to appearance, but judge with righteous judgment" (John 7:24). Jesus commands us to judge righteously, not to abandon discernment.

PM Kimbler

Democratic Talking Point: "Jesus Helped the Poor"

What They Say: "Jesus cared for the poor, so He would support massive government welfare programs and wealth redistribution."

What the Bible Actually Says: "For even when we were with you, we commanded you this: If anyone will not work, neither shall he eat" (2 Thessalonians 3:10). God calls for personal generosity and responsibility, not forced government redistribution.

Democratic Talking Point: "Jesus Welcomed the Stranger"

What They Say: "The Bible commands us to welcome strangers, so we must support open borders and sanctuary cities."

What the Bible Actually Says: "One law shall be for the native-born and for the stranger who dwells among you" (Exodus 12:49). Compassion and law work together, not against each other.

Democratic Talking Point: "God is Love"

What They Say: "Since God is love, He accepts all lifestyles and identities, including LGBTQ+ relationships."

What the Bible Actually Says: "For this is the love of God, that we keep His commandments. And His commandments are not burdensome" (1 John 5:3). God's love is holy love that calls us to righteousness, not affirmation of sin.

Democratic Talking Point: "Separation of Church and State"

What They Say: "Christians should keep their faith private and not impose their beliefs on others through politics."

What the Bible Actually Says: "But Peter and John answered and said to them, 'Whether it is right in the sight of God to listen to you more than to God, you judge'" (Acts 4:19). God's authority extends over all of life, including government and politics.

PM Kimbler

Appendix B: Key Bible Verses for Voting

On the Sanctity of Life

- "Before I formed you in the womb I knew you; before you were born I sanctified you" (Jeremiah 1:5)
- "Whoever sheds man's blood, by man his blood shall be shed; for in the image of God He made man" (Genesis 9:6)
- "Deliver those who are drawn toward death, and hold back those stumbling to the slaughter" (Proverbs 24:11)

On Marriage and Sexuality

- "So God created man in His own image; in the image of God He created him; male and female He created them" (Genesis 1:27)
- "For this reason a man shall leave his father and mother and be joined to his wife, and the two shall become one flesh" (Mark 10:7-8)
- "You shall not lie with a male as with a woman. It is an abomination" (Leviticus 18:22)
- "Marriage is honorable among all, and the bed undefiled; but fornicators and adulterers God will judge" (Hebrews 13:4)

On Work and Economics

- "For even when we were with you, we commanded you this: If anyone will not work, neither shall he eat" (2 Thessalonians 3:10)
- "The rich rules over the poor, and the borrower is servant to the lender" (Proverbs 22:7)
- "Let him labor, working with his hands what is good, that he may have something to give him who has need" (Ephesians 4:28)

On Government Authority

- "Let every soul be subject to the governing authorities. For there is no authority except from God, and the authorities that exist are appointed by God" (Romans 13:1)
- "When the righteous are in authority, the people rejoice; but when a wicked man rules, the people groan" (Proverbs 29:2)
- "Blessed is the nation whose God is the Lord, the people He has chosen as His own inheritance" (Psalm 33:12)

On Justice

- "You shall not show partiality in judgment; you shall hear the small as well as the great; you shall not be afraid in any man's presence, for the judgment is God's" (Deuteronomy 1:17)

- "You shall follow what is altogether just, that you may live and inherit the land which the Lord your God is giving you" (Deuteronomy 16:20)
- "He has shown you, O man, what is good; and what does the Lord require of you but to do justly, to love mercy, and to walk humbly with your God?" (Micah 6:8)

On National Boundaries

- "And He has made from one blood every nation of men to dwell on all the face of the earth, and has determined their pre-appointed times and the boundaries of their dwellings" (Acts 17:26)

On Religious Freedom

- "But Peter and John answered and said to them, 'Whether it is right in the sight of God to listen to you more than to God, you judge'" (Acts 4:19)
- "Declare His glory among the nations, His wonders among all peoples" (Psalm 96:3)

PM Kimbler

Appendix C: Platform Comparison—Democrats vs. Republicans

ABORTION

Democrat Platform 2024[18]:
- Unlimited abortion access through all nine months
- Taxpayer-funded abortions
- No parental consent requirements
- No waiting periods or counseling requirements
- Opposes conscience protections for healthcare workers

Republican Platform 2024[19]:
- Supports protecting unborn life
- Opposes taxpayer funding of abortion
- Supports parental consent laws
- Supports conscience protections
- Appointed Supreme Court justices who overturned Roe v. Wade

Biblical Position: Life begins at conception; God forms us in the womb

MARRIAGE AND FAMILY

Democrat Platform 2024:

- Celebrates same-sex marriage as fundamental right
- Supports transgender ideology in schools
- Promotes "gender-affirming care" for minors
- Mandates preferred pronoun usage
- Undermines parental rights

Republican Platform 2024:

- Supports traditional marriage definition
- Opposes transgender ideology in schools
- Protects parental rights in education
- Supports biological reality in sports and facilities

Biblical Position: Marriage is between one man and one woman; God created male and female

RELIGIOUS LIBERTY

Democrat Platform 2024:

- Promotes "separation" that silences faith
- Supports forcing Christians to violate conscience
- Opposes religious exemptions
- Sides with censorship of biblical views

Republican Platform 2024:
- Protects religious freedom and conscience rights
- Supports faith-based exemptions
- Defends right to practice faith publicly
- Opposes religious discrimination

Biblical Position: We must obey God rather than men; faith is not private

ECONOMIC POLICY

Democrat Platform 2024:
- Massive government spending and debt
- Higher taxes on working families
- Expanded welfare without work requirements
- Government control of healthcare and energy

Republican Platform 2024:
- Lower taxes and limited government
- Supports work requirements for able-bodied adults
- Promotes free market solutions
- Reduces regulatory burden on businesses

Biblical Position: Those who don't work shouldn't eat; avoid debt slavery

PM Kimbler

Appendix D: Resources for Christian Voters

Essential Books

- "The Bible and Government" by Wayne Grudem
- "Politics According to the Bible" by Wayne Grudem
- "How Should We Then Live?" by Francis Schaeffer
- "God and Government" by Charles Colson
- "The Call of Duty" by Richard Land

Key Organizations[20]

Family Research Council (frc.org)

- Policy analysis from biblical perspective
- Voter guides and candidate positions
- Action alerts on key issues

Alliance Defending Freedom[21] (adflegal.org)

- Legal defense of religious liberty
- Updates on court cases affecting faith
- Resources on conscience rights

American Family Association (afa.net)

- Cultural analysis and action alerts
- Boycott information for corporate activism

- Traditional values advocacy

Liberty Counsel (lc.org)

- Legal defense of constitutional freedoms
- Religious liberty litigation
- Policy analysis and advocacy

Susan B. Anthony Pro-Life America[22] (sba-list.org)

- Pro-life candidate endorsements
- Voter mobilization efforts
- Policy analysis on life issues

Websites for Research

Ballotpedia.org - Nonpartisan candidate and issue information **Vote411.org** - League of Women Voters candidate guide **Votesmart.org** - Candidate positions and voting records **GovTrack.us** - Congressional voting records and bill tracking.

Key Questions to Ask Candidates

1. Do you believe life begins at conception?
2. Will you protect religious freedom and conscience rights?
3. Do you support the biblical definition of marriage?
4. Will you defend parental rights in education?

5. Do you believe in limited government under God's authority?

6. Will you protect our national borders?

7. Do you support work requirements for government assistance?

8. Will you defend free speech, including biblical speech?

PM Kimbler

Appendix E: How the Democratic Party Abandoned God

Historical Timeline of Departure
1960s - The Shift Begins

- Removal of prayer from public schools (1962-1963)
- Liberal theology infiltrates mainline denominations
- "God is Dead" movement gains academic support

1970s - Roe v. Wade

- 1973: Supreme Court legalizes abortion
- Democratic Party adopts pro-abortion platform
- Feminist movement redefines traditional family roles

1980s - The Moral Majority Response

- Reagan wins evangelical vote with pro-life, pro-family platform
- Democrats double down on secular progressive agenda
- ACLU lawsuit strategy removes Christian symbols from public spaces

1990s - Culture War Escalates

- "Don't Ask, Don't Tell" military policy
- Partial-birth abortion defended by Democrats

- Hillary Clinton's "It Takes a Village" philosophy undermines family

2000s - Same-Sex Marriage Push

- Massachusetts legalizes same-sex marriage (2003)
- Democratic politicians "evolve" on marriage definition
- Faith-based adoption agencies sued for biblical stance

2010s - Open Hostility to Faith

- Obama administration attacks religious liberty
- Little Sisters of the Poor forced to provide contraceptives
- Christian bakers, photographers, florists targeted for beliefs

2020s - Complete Abandonment

- 2024 Democratic platform omits God entirely
- Transgender ideology imposed on children
- Churches shut down while secular businesses stay open during COVID
- Parents labeled "terrorists" for opposing woke school curricula

Key Platform Changes Over Time

1960 Democratic Platform:

- Acknowledged "Almighty God"

- Supported traditional family values
- Opposed communist atheism

2024 Democratic Platform:
- No mention of God, Lord, or Creator
- Celebrates abortion as "reproductive freedom"
- Promotes transgender ideology
- Attacks religious conscience rights

The Path Forward: What It Will Take

For Individual Christians:
- Stop supporting politicians who oppose God's design
- Vote according to biblical principles, not party loyalty
- Speak truth in love, regardless of social pressure

For Churches:
- Pastors must preach on political issues from biblical perspective
- Churches must educate members on candidate positions
- Christian institutions must maintain biblical standards

For the Nation:

- Christians must engage in politics at every level
- Biblical candidates must run for office
- Prayer and revival must precede political change

Appendix F: Your Biblical Voting Checklist

Before You Vote - Questions for Self-Examination

Personal Preparation: ☐ Have I prayed about my voting choices? ☐ Have I studied what the Bible says about key issues? ☐ Am I voting based on God's Word or my emotions? ☐ Am I willing to be unpopular for biblical truth? ☐ Have I examined candidate positions, not just party labels?

Biblical Issue Positions: ☐ Does this candidate protect unborn life? ☐ Does this candidate support biblical marriage? ☐ Does this candidate defend religious liberty? ☐ Does this candidate promote personal responsibility over government dependency? ☐ Does this candidate support proper role of government under God? ☐ Does this candidate defend parental rights? ☐ Does this candidate protect national sovereignty and borders? ☐ Does this candidate promote justice based on truth, not identity politics?

Candidate Evaluation Scorecard

Rate each candidate on these issues (1-5 scale, 5 being most biblical):

Life Issues:

- Opposes abortion in all circumstances: ____
- Supports adoption and pregnancy centers: ____
- Opposes euthanasia and assisted suicide: ____

Marriage and Family:

- Supports biblical definition of marriage: ____
- Opposes transgender ideology in schools: ____
- Protects parental rights in education: ____
- Opposes sexualization of children: ____

Religious Liberty:

- Protects conscience rights for Christians: ____
- Defends public expression of faith: ____
- Opposes forcing Christians to violate beliefs: ____

Economic Issues:

- Supports work requirements for assistance: ____
- Opposes excessive government spending and debt: ____
- Promotes personal responsibility: ____

Government Role:

- Acknowledges God's authority over government: ____
- Supports limited government: ____
- Defends constitutional freedoms: ____

Total Score: ____/60

Scoring Guide:

- 50-60: Strong biblical candidate
- 40-49: Acceptable with reservations

- 30-39: Significant concerns
- Below 30: Cannot support biblically

Election Day Checklist

☐ I have researched all candidates and ballot measures ☐ I have prayed about my choices ☐ I am voting according to biblical principles, not party loyalty ☐ I am prepared to explain my choices using Scripture ☐ I am voting as an act of worship and obedience to God

After the Election

☐ I will pray for all elected officials, even those I didn't support ☐ I will hold elected officials accountable to biblical standards ☐ I will stay engaged in the political process year-round ☐ I will teach my children about faithful citizenship ☐ I will not compromise biblical truth for political expediency

Resources for Staying Informed

Daily Reading:

- Scripture first, news second
- Christian news sources that apply biblical worldview
- Primary sources (actual voting records, not media spin)

Regular Actions:

- Contact elected officials about biblical issues
- Attend candidate forums and town halls
- Support biblical candidates with time and money
- Engage respectfully with those who disagree

Long-term Commitment:

- Consider running for office yourself
- Mentor other Christians in faithful citizenship
- Support Christian education and worldview training
- Never stop learning how to apply Scripture to cultural issues

Final Reminder

"All Scripture is given by inspiration of God, and is profitable for doctrine, for reproof, for correction, for instruction in righteousness, that the man of God may be complete, thoroughly equipped for every good work" (2 Timothy 3:16-17).

Your vote is one of those "good works" that Scripture equips you for. Vote faithfully. Vote biblically. Vote without compromise.

SCRIPTURE INDEX

Listed in Biblical Order

Genesis

- Genesis 1:27 - So God created man in His own image
- Genesis 2:15 - Then the Lord God took the man and put him in the garden of Eden
- Genesis 2:24 - Therefore a man shall leave his father and mother
- Genesis 5:2 - Male and female He created them, and He blessed them
- Genesis 9:6 - Whoever sheds man's blood, by man his blood shall be shed
- Genesis 41:46-57 - Joseph's wisdom during famine

Exodus

- Exodus 12:49 - One law shall be for the native-born and for the stranger

Leviticus

- Leviticus 18:21 - You shall not let any of your descendants pass through the fire
- Leviticus 18:22 - You shall not lie with a male as with a woman
- Leviticus 19:15 - You shall do no injustice in judgment
- Leviticus 19:34 - The stranger who dwells among you shall be to you as one born among you

Numbers

- Numbers 35:33 - So you shall not pollute the land where you are

Deuteronomy

- Deuteronomy 1:17 - You shall not show partiality in judgment
- Deuteronomy 5:32 - Therefore you shall be careful to do as the Lord your God has commanded you
- Deuteronomy 6:6-7 - And these words which I command you today shall be in your heart
- Deuteronomy 16:20 - You shall follow what is altogether just
- Deuteronomy 22:5 - A woman shall not wear anything that pertains to a man
- Deuteronomy 27:25 - Cursed is the one who takes a bribe to slay an innocent person
- Deuteronomy 32:8 - When the Most High divided their inheritance to the nations

Joshua

- Joshua 24:15 - Choose for yourselves this day whom you will serve

1 Samuel

- 1 Samuel 8 - Israel's demand for a king

1 Kings

- 1 Kings 18:21 - How long will you falter between two opinions?

2 Chronicles

- 2 Chronicles 7:14 - If My people who are called by My name will humble themselves

Psalms

- Psalm 1:2 - But his delight is in the law of the Lord
- Psalm 2:1-3 - Why do the nations rage and the people plot a vain thing?
- Psalm 9:17 - The wicked shall be turned into hell
- Psalm 10:16 - The Lord is King forever and ever
- Psalm 32:5 - I acknowledged my sin to You
- Psalm 33:12 - Blessed is the nation whose God is the Lord
- Psalm 37:28 - For the Lord loves justice
- Psalm 56:11 - In God I have put my trust
- Psalm 96:3 - Declare His glory among the nations
- Psalm 99:4 - The strength of the King loves justice
- Psalm 118:9 - It is better to trust in the Lord than to put confidence in princes
- Psalm 119:1 - Blessed are the undefiled in the way

- Psalm 119:2 - Happy are those who keep His testimonies
- Psalm 119:30 - I have chosen the way of truth
- Psalm 119:46 - I will speak of Your testimonies also before kings
- Psalm 119:89 - Forever, O Lord, Your word is settled in heaven
- Psalm 119:93 - I will never forget Your precepts
- Psalm 119:165 - Great peace have those who love Your law
- Psalm 138:2 - You have magnified Your word above all Your name
- Psalm 139:13-16 - For You formed my inward parts
- Psalm 139:14 - I will praise You, for I am fearfully and wonderfully made

Proverbs

- Proverbs 6:16-17 - These six things the Lord hates
- Proverbs 10:4 - The hand of the diligent will rule
- Proverbs 12:22 - Lying lips are an abomination to the Lord
- Proverbs 14:34 - Righteousness exalts a nation
- Proverbs 21:15 - It is a joy for the just to do justice
- Proverbs 22:7 - The rich rules over the poor

- Proverbs 24:11 - Deliver those who are drawn toward death
- Proverbs 27:5 - Open rebuke is better than love carefully concealed
- Proverbs 28:1 - The wicked flee when no one pursues
- Proverbs 29:2 - When the righteous are in authority, the people rejoice
- Proverbs 29:18 - Where there is no revelation, the people cast off restraint
- Proverbs 29:25 - The fear of man brings a snare
- Proverbs 29:27 - The righteous and the wicked are an abomination to each other

Ecclesiastes
- Ecclesiastes 3:13 - Also that every man should eat and drink and enjoy the good of all his labor

Isaiah
- Isaiah 1:15-17 - When you spread out your hands, I will hide My eyes from you
- Isaiah 1:17 - Learn to do good; seek justice, correct oppression
- Isaiah 5:20 - Woe to those who call evil good and good evil
- Isaiah 40:8 - The grass withers, the flower fades, but the word of our God stands forever

- Isaiah 49:15-16 - Can a woman forget her nursing child?
- Isaiah 51:7 - Listen, O you who know righteousness
- Isaiah 55:7 - Let the wicked forsake his way
- Isaiah 55:8-9 - For My thoughts are not your thoughts

Jeremiah

- Jeremiah 1:5 - Before I formed you in the womb I knew you
- Jeremiah 7:31 - And they have built the high places of Tophet
- Jeremiah 17:5 - Thus says the Lord: Cursed is the man who trusts in man

Daniel

- Daniel 2:21 - And He changes the times and the seasons

Micah

- Micah 6:8 - He has shown you, O man, what is good

Matthew

- Matthew 5:13-14 - You are the salt of the earth
- Matthew 5:19 - Whoever therefore breaks one of the least of these commandments
- Matthew 6:24 - No one can serve two masters
- Matthew 7:21 - Not everyone who says to Me, 'Lord, Lord,' shall enter the kingdom of heaven

- Matthew 10:28 - And do not fear those who kill the body
- Matthew 18:5 - Whoever receives one little child like this in My name receives Me
- Matthew 19:4-6 - Have you not read that He who made them at the beginning
- Matthew 25:14-30 - Parable of the Talents

Mark

- Mark 8:38 - For whoever is ashamed of Me and My words
- Mark 10:6-9 - But from the beginning of the creation, God made them male and female
- Mark 10:14 - Let the little children come to Me
- Mark 12:31 - You shall love your neighbor as yourself

Luke

- Luke 6:46 - But why do you call Me 'Lord, Lord,' and not do the things which I say?
- Luke 10:25-37 - Parable of the Good Samaritan

John

- John 7:24 - Do not judge according to appearance, but judge with righteous judgment
- John 8:31-32 - If you abide in My word, you are My disciples indeed
- John 14:15 - If you love Me, keep My commandments

- John 16:33 - These things I have spoken to you, that in Me you may have peace

Acts

- Acts 4:19 - But Peter and John answered and said to them
- Acts 5:29 - But Peter and the other apostles answered and said: We ought to obey God rather than men
- Acts 17:11 - These were more fair-minded than those in Thessalonica
- Acts 17:26 - And He has made from one blood every nation of men

Romans

- Romans 1:16 - For I am not ashamed of the gospel of Christ
- Romans 1:25 - who exchanged the truth of God for the lie
- Romans 1:26-27 - For this reason God gave them up to vile passions
- Romans 13:1 - Let every soul be subject to the governing authorities

1 Corinthians

- 1 Corinthians 6:11 - And such were some of you
- 1 Corinthians 15:33 - Do not be deceived: Bad company corrupts good character

- 1 Corinthians 16:13 - Watch, stand fast in the faith, be brave, be strong

2 Corinthians

- 2 Corinthians 5:20 - Now then, we are ambassadors for Christ
- 2 Corinthians 9:7 - So let each one give as he purposes in his heart
- 2 Corinthians 13:8 - For we can do nothing against the truth, but for the truth

Galatians

- Galatians 4:16 - Have I therefore become your enemy because I tell you the truth?
- Galatians 5:1 - Stand fast therefore in the liberty by which Christ has made us free

Ephesians

- Ephesians 4:28 - Let him labor, working with his hands what is good
- Ephesians 5:10 - finding out what is acceptable to the Lord
- Ephesians 5:11 - And have no fellowship with the unfruitful works of darkness
- Ephesians 6:17 - And take the helmet of salvation, and the sword of the Spirit

Philippians

- Philippians 1:28 - and not in any way terrified by your adversaries
- Philippians 4:13 - I can do all things through Christ who strengthens me

1 Thessalonians

- 1 Thessalonians 2:4 - But as we have been approved by God to be entrusted with the gospel

2 Thessalonians

- 2 Thessalonians 3:10 - For even when we were with you, we commanded you this

1 Timothy

- 1 Timothy 2:1-2 - Therefore I exhort first of all that supplications, prayers, intercessions

2 Timothy

- 2 Timothy 2:15 - Be diligent to present yourself approved to God
- 2 Timothy 3:16-17 - All Scripture is given by inspiration of God
- 2 Timothy 4:2 - Preach the word! Be ready in season and out of season
- 2 Timothy 4:7 - I have fought the good fight, I have finished the race

Hebrews

- Hebrews 10:25 - not forsaking the assembling of ourselves together
- Hebrews 10:38-39 - Now the just shall live by faith
- Hebrews 13:4 - Marriage is honorable among all

James

- James 1:22 - But be doers of the word, and not hearers only

1 Peter

- 1 Peter 3:14-15 - And do not be afraid of their threats, nor be troubled
- 2 Peter 2:1 - But there were also false prophets among the people

1 John

- 1 John 2:3-4 - Now by this we know that we know Him, if we keep His commandments
- 1 John 5:3 - For this is the love of God, that we keep His commandments

Revelation

- Revelation 2:10 - Be faithful until death, and I will give you the crown of life
- Revelation 3:15-16 - I know your works, that you are neither cold nor hot So then because thou art lukewarm, and neither cold nor hot, I will spue thee out of my mouth."

ENDNOTES

1 Gallup, "Moral Issues," Values and Beliefs Poll, May 2023. Available at: gallup.com/poll/1681/moral-issues.aspx

2 Pew Research Center, "Changing Attitudes on Gay Marriage," Religious Landscape Study, 2023. Available at: pewresearch.org/religion/fact-sheet/changing-attitudes-on-gay-marriage/

3 U.S. Treasury, "Monthly Statement of the Public Debt," December 2024. Available at: treasurydirect.gov/NP/debt/current

4 U.S. Customs and Border Protection, "Southwest Border Land Border Encounters," Fiscal Year 2024. Available at: cbp.gov/newsroom/stats/southwest-land-border-encounters

5 Planned Parenthood Federation of America, "2022-2023 Annual Report." Available at: plannedparenthood.org/annual-report

6 Centers for Disease Control and Prevention, "Abortion Surveillance — United States, 2021," MMWR Surveillance Summaries, November 2024.

7 Guttmacher Institute, "Induced Abortion in the United States," September 2019. Available at: guttmacher.org/fact-sheet/induced-abortion-united-states

8 Margaret Sanger, "The Pivot of Civilization" (New York: Brentano's, 1922), Chapter 8.

9 National Right to Life Committee, "Abortion Statistics: United States Data and Trends," 2024. Available at: nrlc.org/uploads/factsheets/FS01AbortionInTheUS.pdf

10 Georgia Bureau of Investigation, "Laken Riley Murder Case," February 2024 press release.

11 Houston Police Department, "Jocelyn Nungaray Murder Investigation," June 2024 press release.

12 Harford County Sheriff's Office, "Kayla Hamilton Murder Case," January 2022 press release.

13 U.S. Department of Health and Human Services, Office of Inspector General, "The Office of Refugee Resettlement's Efforts to Serve Unaccompanied Alien Children," Report A-12-18-20028, August 2019.

14 VAERS (Vaccine Adverse Event Reporting System), Centers for Disease Control and Prevention. Available at: vaers.hhs.gov/data.html

15 OpenVAERS, "COVID Vaccine Adverse Event Reports." Available at: openvaers.com/covid-data

16 U.S. Census Bureau, "Quick Facts: Arizona." Available at: census.gov/quickfacts/AZ

17 Various news reports from Fox News, CNN, New York Times, Washington Post regarding specific political figures' actions during COVID-19, 2020-2022.

18 Democratic National Committee, "2024 Democratic Party Platform." Available at: democrats.org/where-we-stand/party-platform/

19 Republican National Committee, "2024 Republican Party Platform." Available at: gop.com/platform/

[20] Family Research Council, "Voter Guide 2024: Key Issues for Christian Voters." Available at: frc.org/voterguide

[21] Alliance Defending Freedom, "Religious Liberty Cases Database." Available at: adflegal.org/issues/religious-freedom

[22] Susan B. Anthony Pro-Life America, "2024 Election Analysis." Available at: sba-list.org/2024-analysis

[23] American College of Pediatricians, "Gender Identity Disorder in Children," August 2016. Available at: acpeds.org/position-statements/gender-identity-disorder-in-children

[24] Heritage Foundation, "2024 Index of Economic Freedom." Available at: heritage.org/index/

[25] Cato Institute, "Economic Freedom of the World: 2024 Annual Report." Available at: cato.org/economic-freedom-world

[26] Congressional Budget Office, "The Budget and Economic Outlook: 2024 to 2034," February 2024. Available at: cbo.gov/publication/59710

The harvest is plentiful, but the workers are few. Now go and make disciples of men. God Bless.

www.ingramcontent.com/pod-product-compliance
Lightning Source LLC
Chambersburg PA
CBHW020500030426
42337CB00011B/171